P9-DYY-754

READING GROUP CHOICES

2020

Selections for lively discussions

Reading Group Choices' goal is to join with publishers, bookstores, libraries, trade associations, and authors to develop resources to enhance the shared reading group experience. *Reading Group Choices* is distributed annually to bookstores, libraries, and directly to book groups. Titles included in the current and previous issues are posted on ReadingGroupChoices.com. Books presented here have been recommended by book group members, librarians, booksellers, literary agents, publicists, authors, and publishers. All submissions are then reviewed to ensure the discussibility of each title. Once a title is approved for inclusion, publishers are asked to underwrite production costs so that copies of *Reading Group Choices* can be distributed for a minimal charge. For additional copies, you can place an order through our online store, contact us, or contact your local library or bookstore. For more information, please visit our website at **ReadingGroupChoices.com.**

Cover art, *Paper Escape* by Rachel Grant (2017)
Design by Sarah Jane Boecher

Copyright © 2019 Reading Group Choices LLC

All Rights Reserved.

Published in the United States by Reading Group Choices LLC

ISBN 9781733268301

For further information, contact:
Reading Group Choices
info@ReadingGroupChoices.com
ReadingGroupChoices.com

PRAISE FOR *READING GROUP CHOICES*

"We have learned over the years that displays are a great way to encourage circulation at our small, rural library. One of our best displays is based on the wonderful literary guide published by Reading Group Choices! ... Patrons cannot wait to get their copies and start reading. We sincerely LOVE your product and feel that it helps us create one of our favorite displays EVER."
—**Gail Nartker, Sandusky District Library**

"Reading Group Choices continues to be a first-rate guide for those delicious reads that book group members enjoy reading, and that prompt the most enriching discussions." —**Donna Paz Kaufman, Paz & Associates, The Bookstore Training Group**

"I recommend Reading Group Choices as the number one starting point for book clubs. The newsletter is fantastic, and I especially like the Spotlight Book Club section. It is a nice way to meet other book clubs. I am very happy with the book selections offered by Reading Group Choices. Thank you for this excellent service." —**Ana Martin, Cover to Cover Book Club, Hollywood, FL**

"Not only is Reading Group Choices a great resource for individual readers and book groups, it's also an invaluable tool for teachers looking to introduce new books into their curriculum. Reading Group Choices is a brilliant concept, well executed." —**Kathleen Rourke, Executive Director of Educational Sales and Marketing, Candlewick Press**

"I love your book, website and the newsletters! As an organizer of two book clubs, it's so great to get an early line on upcoming titles. The hardest part is waiting so long to read the book! By using recommendations from your newsletters, I can build a list of monthly book selections one whole year in advance." —**Marcia, CCSI Book Club**

"Quail Ridge Books has worked with Reading Group Choices for many years and the guide has been sought out at our twice yearly Book Club Bash. The prize bags of books have been a highlight. We are great partners in getting good books into the hands of people who love to read and discuss books."
—**René Martin, Events Coordinator, Quail Ridge Books**

Welcome to

READING GROUP
CHOICES

"*I believe art is utterly important. It is one of the things that could save us.*"

"*Words have not only a definition ... but also the felt quality of their own kind of sound.*"

—Mary Oliver (1935-2019)

Dear Readers,

Welcome to the 26th edition of *Reading Group Choices*! We are wrapping up a quarter century and starting a new one. Thank you to all of our readers who inspire and challenge us to find and recommend new books each year. We listened to your requests and searched for titles from around the globe.

The 26th edition includes enjoyable, unique, and challenging fiction, nonfiction, and young adult titles, which we chose specifically to inspire thoughtful and lively conversation. Some of the titles will be published in 2020 so you can plan ahead too.

There are longer versions of the conversation starters available online in our searchable database. Be sure to sign up for our eNewsletter where you can find out about monthly recommendations and giveaways as well as other fun resources for your groups.

To order more copies of this edition or past editions you can visit our store online at ReadingGroupChoices.com, or mail in the order form at the back of this book.

We hope you enjoy another year of reading, discussing, and discovering new favorite books!

Mary Morgan
Reading Group Choices

Contents

YOUNG ADULT

FICTION

THE BOOK WOMAN OF TROUBLESOME CREEK

Kim Michele Richardson

The hardscrabble folks of Troublesome Creek have to scrap for everything—everything except books, that is. Thanks to Roosevelt's Kentucky Pack Horse Library Project, Troublesome's got its very own traveling librarian, Cussy Mary Carter.

Cussy's not only a book woman, however, she's also the last of her kind, her skin a shade of blue unlike most anyone else. Not everyone is keen on Cussy's family or the Library Project, and a Blue is often blamed for any whiff of trouble. If Cussy wants to bring the joy of books to the hill folks, she's going to have to confront prejudice as old as the Appalachias and suspicion as deep as the holler.

"A lush love letter to the redemptive power of books." —**Joshilyn Jackson**, *New York Times* and *USA Today* bestselling author

"Fascinating … impressive storytelling." —**Ron Rash**, *New York Times* bestselling author

"Richardson has penned an emotionally moving and fascinating story." —*BookPage*

"A hauntingly atmospheric love letter to the first mobile library in Kentucky and the fierce, brave packhorse librarians who wove their way from shack to shack dispensing literacy, hope, and—just as importantly—a compassionate human connection." —**Sara Gruen**, author of *Water for Elephants*

"As beautiful and honest as it is fierce and heartwrenching." —**Karen Abbott**, *New York Times* bestelling author

ABOUT THE AUTHOR: **Kim Michele Richardson** was born in Kentucky and resides part-time in Western North Carolina. Her works include *Liar's Bench*, *GodPretty in the Tobacco Field* and *The Sisters of Glass Ferry*. *The Book Woman of Troublesome Creek* is her fourth novel.

May 2019 | Hardcover | $25.99 | 9781492691631 | Sourcebooks Landmark
May 2019 | Paperback | $15.99 | 9781492671527 | Sourcebooks Landmark

CONVERSATION STARTERS

1. How has a librarian or booklover impacted your life? Have you ever connected with a book or author in a meaningful way? Explain.

2. Missionaries, government, social workers, and various religious groups have always visited eastern Kentucky to reform, modernize, and mold hillfolk to their acceptable standards. Do you think Cussy faced this kind of prejudice from the outside world? Is there any prejudice or stigma associated with the people of Appalachia today?

3. How do you think Cussy's father feels after he marries her off to an abusive man? Why do you think he agrees to Charlie Frazier's proposal in the first place? What do you imagine life was like for an unwed woman at that time?

4. When Cussy receives the cure for her blueness from Doc, she realizes there's a price to pay for her white skin, and the side effects soon become too much to handle. If you were in Cussy's shoes, would you sacrifice your health for a chance at "normalcy"? If there weren't any side effects, do you think Cussy would have continued to take the medication? Would you?

5. Cussy has to deal with the loss of many loved ones in a very short amount of time. How do you think she handles her grief? Which loss was the most difficult for you to read?

6. What do you think life was like for the people of Troublesome? What are some of the highlights of living in such a remote place? What are some of the challenges the people on Cussy's library route face?

7. What do you think happens to Cussy, Jackson, Honey, and the other inhabitants of Troublesome after the story ends? Imagine you were Cussy. How would you feel leaving Troublesome for good?

CHRONICLES OF A RADICAL HAG (WITH RECIPES)

Lorna Landvik

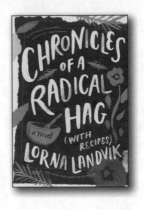

When Haze Evans first appeared in the *Granite Creek Gazette*, she earned fans by writing a story about her bachelor uncle who brought a Queen of the Rodeo to Thanksgiving dinner. Now, fifty years later, when the beloved columnist suffers a massive stroke and falls into a coma, publisher Susan McGrath fills the void (temporarily, she hopes) with Haze's past columns. Framed by news stories of half a century and annotated with the town's chorus of voices, Haze's story unfolds, as do those of others touched by the *Granite Creek Gazette*, including Susan, struggling with her troubled marriage, and her teenage son Sam, who—much to his surprise—enjoys his summer job reading the paper archives and discovers secrets that have been locked in the files for decades, along with sad and surprising truths about Haze's past.

With her customary warmth and wit, Lorna Landvik summons a lifetime at once lost and recovered, a complicated past that speaks with knowing eloquence to a confused present. Topical yet timeless, *Chronicles of a Radical Hag* reminds us—sometimes with a subtle touch, sometimes with gobsmacking humor—of the power of words and of silence, as well as the wonder of finding in each other what we never even knew we were missing.

"At a time when local newspapers are nearing extinction, and reporters are deemed enemies of the people, Landvik's smart and lovely paean to journalists is a welcome reminder of the important role they play in the lives of those who depend on newspapers for more than just information." —**Booklist**

"Landvik's heartwarming novel is packed with big-hearted people tenderly and hilariously learning to appreciate the past and each other." —**Star Tribune**

"A comic love letter to journalism and literature, Lorna Landvik's newest novel is smart, funny, and intimate, with a terrifically memorable cast of small-town characters. Read the book, then head for the kitchen and start baking. Delicious!" —**Julie Schumacher, author of *The Shakespeare Requirement***

ABOUT THE AUTHOR: **Lorna Landvik** is the best-selling author of twelve novels, including *Patty Jane's House of Curl* and *Once in a Blue Moon Lodge*. She has performed stand-up and improvisational comedy around the country and is a public speaker, playwright, and actor.

March 2019 | Hardcover | $25.95 | 9781517905996 | University of Minnesota Press

CONVERSATION STARTERS

1. Haze had a hard time thinking of her column name—what would yours be, and what would the focus of your columns be?

2. Are you a newspaper reader, or do you rely on the Internet for your news? Do you think one's better than the other?

3. Who are some columnists/bloggers whose work you regularly read, and why?

4. What do you think of Haze's love affair and how she justified it?

5. Susan and Sam were shocked by the revelations of Haze's love affair—have you ever learned of a family secret that's shocked or surprised you?

6. Sam's teacher begins a "Radical Hag Wednesday" to interest her students in Haze's columns and the opinions expressed therein. What did your favorite teacher do to interest the class in the subject they were teaching?

7. What do you think the role of a free press in today's society is, and what do you think of our American media?

8. Susan's high-powered career had a role in her marriage troubles. In your own partnership, how is work life/home life balanced?

9. Sam and his friends are inspired by Haze's words to fight for their future. Are you hopeful for young people's future? Why or why not?

10. One of Haze's readers, Joseph Snell, often writes the paper to disparage her columns. Why do you think some people are threatened by others whose opinions differ from their own?

11. Today's online trolls, protected by anonymity, can be vicious. Have you had experience with any of these trolls in your social media postings, and if so, how do you deal with them? What do you think has contributed to the deep decline in civility?

12. What are some of your work experiences dealing with the -isms Haze has to deal with: sexism and ageism?

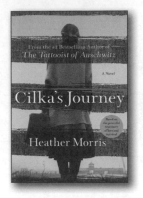

CILKA'S JOURNEY
Heather Morris

Cilka is just sixteen years old when she is taken to Auschwitz-Birkenau Concentration Camp, in 1942. The Commandant at Birkenau, Schwarzhuber, notices her long beautiful hair, and forces her separation from the other women prisoners. Cilka learns quickly that power, even unwillingly given, equals survival.

After liberation, Cilka is charged as a collaborator for sleeping with the enemy and sent to Siberia. But what choice did she have? And where did the lines of morality lie for Cilka, who was sent to Auschwitz when still a child?

In a Siberian prison camp, Cilka faces challenges both new and horribly familiar, including the unwanted attention of the guards. But when she makes an impression on a woman doctor, Cilka is taken under her wing. Cilka begins to tend to the ill in the camp, struggling to care for them under brutal conditions.

Cilka finds endless resources within herself as she daily confronts death and faces terror. And when she nurses a man called Ivan, Cilka finds that despite everything that has happened to her, there is room in her heart for love.

"She was the bravest person I ever met." —**Lale Sokolov on Cilka Klein,** *The Tattooist of Auschwitz*

ABOUT THE AUTHOR: **Heather Morris** is a native of New Zealand, now resident in Australia. For several years, while working in a large public hospital in Melbourne, she studied and wrote screenplays, one of which was optioned by an Academy Award-winning screenwriter in the US. In 2003, Heather was introduced to an elderly gentleman who 'might just have a story worth telling'. Their friendship grew and Lale embarked on a journey of self-scrutiny, entrusting the innermost details of his life during the Holocaust to her. Heather originally wrote Lale's story as a screenplay – which ranked high in international competitions – before reshaping it into her debut novel, *The Tattooist of Auschwitz*.

October 2019 | Hardcover | $27.99 | 9781250265708 | St. Martin's Press

CONVERSATION STARTERS

1. After reading the author's note about her conversation with Lale Sokolov, the Tattooist of Auschwitz, did knowing that Cilka's story is based on a real person change your reading experience? Does the author weave fact and realistic fiction into the story effectively? In what ways?

2. What drew you to this time period and novel? What can humanity still learn from this historical space—from the front lines of an infamous concentration camp to the brutal Russian Gulags?

3. "What you are doing, Cilka, is the only form of resistance you have—staying alive. You are the bravest person I have ever known, I hope you know that." (Chapter 32) Is Lale right? Is Cilka brave, and were her acts of resistance the best course of action she had? What does Cilka feel guilty about or complicit in? How is she suffering because of it?

4. "Another number. Cilka subconsciously rubs her left arm; hidden under her clothing is her identity from that other place. How many times can one person be reduced, erased?" (Chapter 3) How would you answer Cilka here? What inner fire allows Cilka to live? How does she endure with so much death and suffering around her?

5. Does Cilka assume a protective role for the women in her hut? For her block at the camp? In what ways is Cilka a target for their rage and a focus for their hopes for life beyond the fencing? How does she help the women survive the toughest parts of their sentences (the rapes, work, injuries, separation)?

6. Why do the women invest their time and scarce energies into "beautifying" the hut with their meager resources? What does this tell us about the human spirit?

7. In what ways is Cilka's time served in the maternity ward a turning point? How does she intervene with her patients and make a difference? How does she put herself at risk?

8. How does Cilka find her calling with her ambulance work? How did she spur others to be their best selves?

9. Why does Cilka ultimately tell her hut-mates about her experiences and actions at Auschwitz? How does she know the time is right?

10. Why are women's voices of wartime so important to unearth and tell? What could be lost when they are unreported or underreported?

CIRCE
Madeline Miller

The #1 *New York Times* Best Seller

The daring, dazzling and highly anticipated follow-up to *The Song of Achilles*, which brilliantly reimagines the life of Circe, formidable sorceress of *The Odyssey*.

In the house of Helios, god of the sun and mightiest of the Titans, a daughter is born. But Circe is a strange child—not powerful, like her father, nor viciously alluring like her mother. Turning to the world of mortals for companionship, she discovers that she does possess power—the power of witchcraft, which can transform rivals into monsters and menace the gods themselves.

Threatened, Zeus banishes her to a deserted island, where she hones her occult craft, tames wild beasts and crosses paths with many of the most famous figures in all of mythology, including the Minotaur, Daedalus and his doomed son Icarus, the murderous Medea, and, of course, wily Odysseus.

But there is danger, too, for a woman who stands alone, and Circe unwittingly draws the wrath of both men and gods, ultimately finding herself pitted against one of the most terrifying and vengeful of the Olympians. To protect what she loves most, Circe must summon all her strength and choose, once and for all, whether she belongs with the gods she is born from, or the mortals she has come to love.

With unforgettably vivid characters, mesmerizing language and page-turning suspense, *Circe* is a triumph of storytelling, an intoxicating epic of family rivalry, palace intrigue, love and loss, as well as a celebration of indomitable female strength in a man's world.

ABOUT THE AUTHOR: **Madeline Miller** was born in Boston and attended Brown University where she earned her BA and MA in Classics. She lives in Narbeth, PA with her husband and two children. *The Song of Achilles* was awarded the Orange Prize for Fiction and has been translated into twenty-five languages.

April 2018 | Hardcover | $27.00 | 9870316556347 | Little, Brown and Company
January 2020 | Paperback | $ 16.99 | 9870316556323 | Little, Brown and Company

CONVERSATION STARTERS

1. Circe struggles to find a place for herself as a woman in a man's world. What parts of her experience resonate with modern day challenges that women face?

2. A central theme of Homer's *Odyssey* is a longing for "nostos"— homecoming. In what way does that theme resonate with Circe's story?

3. How does Circe's encounter with Prometheus change her? How does it continue to affect her actions?

4. Throughout the novel Circe draws distinctions between gods and mortals. How are each of them portrayed? How does Glaucus change when he becomes a god?

5. Circe wonders if parents can ever see their children clearly. She notes that so often when looking at our children "we see only the mirror of our own faults." What parts of herself does she see when she looks at Telegonus? What are her strengths and weaknesses as a parent to him?

6. Circe's sister Pasiphaë begins the novel as a major antagonist. How does our perspective of her change after Circe's visit to Crete?

7. Circe begins the novel feeling very close to her baby brother Aeëtes. Why do their paths diverge so wildly? Why do you think he make the choices he does?

8. Circe tells us that she recognizes parts of herself in Medea. In what ways are the two women similar? In what ways are they different?

9. Circe says to Telemachus "Do not try to take my regret from me." What does she mean by that? How has her regret shaped her?

10. There are numerous references to crafts in the novel, including weaving, carpentry and metal-working. What role does craft play in Circe's story?

11. How does Circe's relationship with her father change over the course of the book? What do you make of their final conversation?

12. We see numerous powerful characters abusing their positions throughout the story. Are power and abuse necessarily connected? Are there any models for power without cruelty?

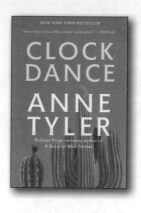

CLOCK DANCE
Anne Tyler

A charming novel of self-discovery and second chances from the Pulitzer Prize-winning author of *A Spool of Blue Thread*

Willa Drake has had three opportunities to start her life over: in 1967, as a schoolgirl whose mother has suddenly disappeared; in 1977, when considering a marriage proposal; and in 1997, as a young widow trying to hold her family together. So she is surprised when in 2017 she is given one last chance to change everything, after receiving a startling phone call from a stranger. Without fully understanding why, she flies across the country to Baltimore to help a young woman she's never met. This impulsive decision, maybe the first one she's consciously made in her life, will lead Willa into uncharted territory—surrounded by eccentric neighbors who treat each other like family, she finds solace and fulfillment in unexpected places. A bewitching novel of hope and transformation, *Clock Dance* gives us Anne Tyler at the height of her powers.

"Exquisite. ... What keeps us glued are the lovely, intricate details; the depiction of human emotion as odd and splendid; and the tiny flickers of hope that feel like bursts of joy." —O, **The Oprah Magazine**

"Tenderly devastating ... Affecting ... A quiet but sharply feminist statement." —**Entertainment Weekly**

"A psychologically astute study of an intelligent, curious woman ... A triumph." —**Boston Globe**

ABOUT THE AUTHOR: **Anne Tyler** is the author of more than twenty novels. Her eleventh novel, *Breathing Lessons*, was awarded the Pulitzer Prize in 1988. She lives in Baltimore, MD.

April 2019 | Paperback | $16.95 | 9780525563020 | Vintage

CONVERSATION STARTERS

1. Why do you think Anne Tyler began the story where she did? What do we learn about Willa by first meeting her as a little girl?

2. What do you make of the stranger on the plane? How would you respond in Willa's position? In Derek's? Have you ever had an experience that felt like this one? How did you want your family and friends to react?

3. Why do you think the cactus is so important to Willa? Are there symbols or landmarks in your own life that give you such powerful feelings?

4. If the book were instead focused on the life of another main character or Baltimore neighbor, which one would you most like to read about? What would their personal journey be?

5. Compare Willa's two marriages, as well as her feelings towards her sons. How has caring for different men shaped her life? How do you think these relationships affect the choices she makes in the second half of the book?

6. Now that you've finished, why do you think the author chose these particular moments in Willa's life to highlight? How do they make her the person she becomes, and where do you think she ends up?

THE CURRENT
Tim Johnston

"Gripping ... Johnston's masterful novel is worth lingering over—it soars above the constraints of a traditional thriller." —People

In the dead of winter outside a small Minnesota town, state troopers pull two young women from an icy river. Only one, Audrey, survives. What happened was no accident, and news of the crime awakens the community's memories of another young woman who lost her life in the same river ten years earlier, a murder that was never solved. Determined to find answers in both crimes, Audrey soon realizes that she's connected to the earlier unsolved case by more than just a river, and the deeper she plunges into her own investigation, the closer she comes to dangerous truths, and to the violence that simmers just below the surface of her hometown.

Grief, suspicion, the innocent and the guilty—all stir to life in this cold northern town where a young woman can come home, but still not be safe.

"Past and present merge in The Current, *Tim Johnston's atmospheric, exquisitely suspenseful novel of two murders separated by 10 years ... a first-rate thriller." —The Washington Post*

"Johnston writes in gracefully exact language with genuine heart ... Reminiscent of writers like Annie Proulx and Richard Bausch." —The New York Times Book Review

"Tim Johnston's second novel, The Current, *is even better than his first, which is saying something. He's a terrific writer and definitely a name to watch." —Dennis Lehane, author of Since We Fell*

"Pick up Tim Johnston's suspenseful novel The Current *and you risk finding yourself glued to your chair ... elegant, cinematic." —Minneapolis Star-Tribune*

ABOUT THE AUTHOR: **Tim Johnston**, a native of Iowa City, is the author of the *New York Times* bestseller *Descent*, as well as a young adult novel, *Never So Green*, and the story collection *Irish Girl*, winner of the Katherine Anne Porter Prize in Short Fiction.

January 2019 | Hardcover | $27.95 | 9781616206772 | Algonquin Books
November 2019 | Paperback | $16.95 | 9781616209834 | Algonquin Books

CONVERSATION STARTERS

1. How would you describe Audrey and Caroline's friendship when the two young women set off for Minnesota? By the time they are plunging toward the Black Root River, have your feelings about them changed?

2. After a tense opening chapter set in the present, the novel transitions to explore the past, dealing with the murder of Holly Burke in the same Black Root River, and with her relationship at the time with Danny Young. Other than the involvement of Audrey's father, the ex-sheriff, what connections did you make between the two crimes?

3. Audrey seems to experience the sense of encountering Caroline and other girls under the water; at one point she even seems to speak with Caroline under the ice. What do you feel these visions mean to Audrey? What do they mean to you, and to your reading of this novel?

4. In what ways does the title of this novel connect to the story, beyond the current of the river?

5. Both Danny Young and his ex-girlfriend, Katie Goss, have been keeping individual secrets for ten years. What has changed to cause Katie to consider coming forward now? And why do you think Danny hid the piece of fabric for ten years?

6. For a book with so many crimes, there seems to be little absolute certainty as to guilt. If you were on the jury that heard these cases, and you had no more evidence than what the author provides with which to convict, how would you decide?

7. Though completed more than a year before the rise of #MeToo, many of the themes in the novel speak to the causes behind that movement. Do you feel the novel contains an accurate representation of the attitudes that brought about the changes in how we discuss male/female relationships today?

8. If you were to encounter any of these characters in another ten years, do you think you would find them greatly changed, or would they still be held in the grip of their pasts?

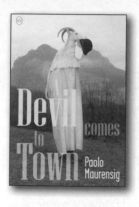

A DEVIL COMES TO TOWN
Paolo Maurensig

Wild rabies runs rampant through the woods. The foxes are gaining ground, boldly making their way into the village. In Dichtersruhe, an insular yet charming haven stifled by the Swiss mountains, these omens go unnoticed by all but the new parish priest. The residents have other things on their mind: Literature. Everyone's a writer—the nights are alive with reworked manuscripts. So when the devil turns up in a black car claiming to be a hot-shot publisher, unsatisfied authorial desires are unleashed and the village's former harmony is shattered. Taut with foreboding and Gothic suspense, Paolo Maurensig gives us a refined and engaging literary parable on narcissism, vainglory, and our inextinguishable thirst for stories.

*"This nested narrative is an entertaining exploration of the manifold powers –creative, confessional, corrupting–of fiction." —**Publisher's Weekly***

*"Maurensig gives us a masterfully constructed gothic horror story designed to keep aspiring writers up at night. A macabre little Alpine horror story elevated by masterful storytelling and language." —**Kirkus***

*"It's a huge amount of fun to be taken on a journey by an unreliable narrator … A Devil Comes to Town is a brilliant form of torture" —**The Literary Review***

ABOUT THE AUTHOR: **Paolo Maurensig** was born in Gorizo, and lives in Udine, Italy. Now a bestselling author, he debuted in 1993 with *The Lüneburg Variation*, translated into twenty-five languages, and selling over 2 million copies in Italy. His novels include *Canone Inverso*, *The Guardian of Dreams*, and *The Archangel of Chess*. For his novel *Theory of Shadows*, published by FSG in the US in January 2018, he won the Bagutta Prize. *A Devil Comes to Town* is his latest novel.

May 2019 | Paperback | $14.99 | 9781642860139 | World Editions

CONVERSATION STARTERS

1. How does the form of the book reflect the themes of the story?

2. Foxes recur frequently in the novel, what is the significance of this? What does the fox represent?

3. Why do you think everybody in Dichtersruhe wants to write a book? What are they hoping to achieve? What is the message?

4. How might you interpret the death of the priest at the end of the novel?

5. Anonymity is a recurring theme in the novel: "the message in the bottle," "the devil in the drawer," "the death of the author," "the unfinished manuscript." What are your thoughts on this? Who owns a text once it has been written?

6. What do you think the author is trying to say about narcissism? Do you agree?

7. Why is the priest the only person to "see" the devil for what he is?

8. What do you think is the importance of the character Marta, the "mentally retarded" daughter of the widow Bauer who wins the Goethe Prize?

9. Goethe himself plays a significant role in the village: what meanings can be deduced from this?

10. The more the villagers write, the more the village itself falls apart, "tourism languishes," etc. What do you think Maurensig is trying to say about literature? Do you agree?

11. In what ways were you able to identify with the characters? Was there one which stood out in this regard?

12. Do you think this is a serious book, a comedy, a satire, a thriller, something else? Why?

13. Did you come away from this book wanting to read more by this author or in this style?

14. How does Maurensig build suspense in the story? In what ways is this effective?

15. How do you view the priest? Is he a good and innocent man? Why does he leave his own manuscript to be found?

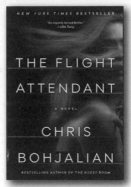

THE FLIGHT ATTENDANT
Chris Bohjalian

A *New York Times*, *Wall Street Journal*, *USA Today* and National Indiebound Best Seller

From the author of *The Guest Room*, a powerful story about the ways an entire life can change in one night: A flight attendant wakes up in the wrong hotel, in the wrong bed, with a dead man— and no idea what happened.

Set amid the captivating world of those whose lives unfold at forty thousand feet, *The Flight Attendant* unveils a spellbinding story of memory, of the giddy pleasures of alcohol, and the devastating consequences of addiction, and of murder far from home.

"Filled with turbulence and sudden plunges in altitude, The Flight Attendant *is a very rare thriller whose penultimate chapter made me think to myself, 'I didn't see that coming.' The novel—Bohjalian's 20th— is also enhanced by his deftness in sketching out vivid characters and locales and by his obvious research into the realities of airline work."* —**Maureen Corrigan**, *The Washington Post*

"Bohjalian is an unfaltering storyteller who crosses genres with fluidity, from historical fiction to literary thrillers...a read-in-one-sitting escapade that is as intellectually satisfying as it is emotionally entertaining." —*Booklist* (**starred review**)

"A magnificent book ... sleek and gorgeous ... This is a Master Class in fiction." —**Augusten Burroughs**

ABOUT THE AUTHOR: **Chris Bohjalian** is the author of twenty books, including *The Guest Room*; *Close Your Eyes, Hold Hands*; *The Sandcastle Girls*; *Skeletons at the Feast*; *The Double Bind*; and *Midwives* which was a number one *New York Times* bestseller and a selection of Oprah's Book Club.

January 2019 | Paperback | $16.00 | 9780525432685 | Vintage

CONVERSATION STARTERS

1. What traits do Cassie and Elena ("Miranda") have in common, and what are their fundamental differences? Though they were raised worlds apart, how did their parents teach them to conceal their true selves? To what extent do both women manage to deceive themselves as well?

2. How did your opinion of Alex Sokolov shift as his life story unfolded? At first, what did you think was the motive behind his murder?

3. How is Cassie's dependence on alcohol linked to her dependence on lying? What is at the root of her cycle of intoxicated euphoria followed by self-loathing?

4. What accounts for the very different paths Cassie and her younger sister, Rosemary, take in life? How does their relationship compare to the one between you and your siblings?

5. What does *The Flight Attendant* say about the distinction between bad decisions and destiny? To what degree are Cassie and Elena in control of their misdirected choices?

6. When Cassie compulsively pilfers items while traveling and then wraps them up as gifts, is she simply trying to live on a limited budget, or does it say something deeper about her relationship to possessions and the images she wanted her loved ones to have of her?

7. As the flight attendants in the novel work a variety of international routes, what do their experiences prove about the common threads that exist in all of humanity, no matter where we are?

8. What are the hallmarks of this author's storytelling? How was your experience of *The Flight Attendant* enhanced by the Bohjalian novels you've previously read?

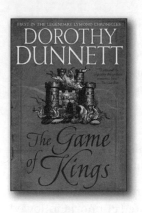

THE GAME OF KINGS: BOOK ONE IN THE LEGENDARY LYMOND CHRONICLES
Dorothy Dunnett

Combining all the political intrigue of *Game of Thrones* with the sweeping romanticism of *Outlander*, Dorothy Dunnett's legendary Lymond Chronicles have enthralled readers for decades and amassed legions of devoted fans. The first book in the series introduces Dunnett's unforgettable antihero as he returns to Scotland with a wild plan to redeem his reputation and save his home.

The year is 1547. Scotland is clinging to independence after a humiliating English invasion. Paradoxically, the country's freedom may depend on a man who stands accused of treason. He is Francis Crawford of Lymond, a scapegrace nobleman of crooked felicities and murderous talents, with a scholar's erudition and a wicked tongue. Clawing his way back into a country that has outlawed him, and to a family that has turned its back on him, Lymond will prove that he has both the will and the cunning to clear his name and defend his people--no matter the cost.

"A masterpiece of historical fiction." —The Washington Post

"First-rate ... suspenseful ... Her hero, in his rococo fashion, is as polished and perceptive as Lord Peter Wimsey and as resourceful as James Bond." —The New York Times Book Review

"Ingenious and exceptional ... its effect brilliant, its pace swift and colorful and its multi-linear plot spirited and absorbing." —Boston Herald

ABOUT THE AUTHOR: **Dorothy Dunnett** was born in Dunfermline, Scotland. She is the author of the Lymond Chronicles; the House of Niccolò novels; seven mysteries; *King Hereafter*, an epic novel about Macbeth; and the text of *The Scottish Highlands*, a book of photographs by David Paterson, on which she collaborated with her husband, Sir Alastair Dunnett. In 1992 she was made an Officer of the Order of the British Empire for services to literature. Lady Dunnett died in 2001.

May 2019 | Paperback | $18.00 | 9780525565246 | Vintage

CONVERSATION STARTERS

1. *The Game of Kings* is the first of six books in the Lymond series based on the imagery of chess. Who would you say are the gamesters in this novel? Do the kings "play" the game or are they pieces in the game? Given the way suspense is created and information hidden, how is the novelist at some level engaged in a chess game with the reader?

2. The brothers Francis Crawford of Lymond and Richard Crawford of Culter appear to be rivals in every field: love, war, politics, family. Which scenes make you feel you've seen the heart of this relationship? Has Dorothy Dunnett managed to create in Richard a character with a fullness of his own, aside from his function as "foil" to Lymond? Is Richard as "romantic" a character as his brother? More romantic?

3. Lymond's Spanish disguise at Hume Castle is only the most theatrical and public of the flamboyant hero's many masquerades; what are some of the others? Besides the multiple political or military purposes, what do you think are some of the deeper psychological reasons for Lymond's brilliance at, or even addiction to, "acting"?

4. Lymond likens sixteenth-century Scotland to a wren caught between crocodiles. How do the character and choices of Wat Scott of Buccleuch mirror, and affect, what's happening in Scotland? What about Andrew Hunter of Ballaggan? Would you call Agnes Herries, later Maxwell, such a "wren"?

5. Perhaps the most poignant relationship in the novel is that between the protagonist, Lymond, and young Will Scott, the heir to the lordship of Buccleuch. What are some of the lessons Will must learn during his "apprenticeship" with Lymond?

6. Startlingly enough, in the course of this novel the glamorous and dangerous protagonist has no lovers and no sex, delivers only one kiss, and ends up in the embrace of his mother. What are some of the ironies here? What does the romantic triangle created between Richard Crawford, his wife Mariotta, and Francis Crawford seem to be saying about "romance"? About love?

7. Why does Lymond put himself in the hands of his enemies to redeem Christian Stewart, held hostage in England? How is this relationship, as Lymond says, "made possible" by her blindness? How does the blind girl help the reader more truly "see" Lymond?

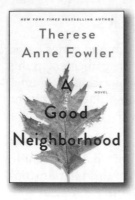

A GOOD NEIGHBORHOOD
Therese Anne Fowler

With little in common except a property line, these two very different families quickly find themselves at odds: first, over an historic oak tree, and soon after, the blossoming romance between their two teenagers. Told in multiple points of view, *A Good Neighborhood* asks big questions about life in America today — what does it mean to be a good neighbor? How do we live alongside each other when we don't see eye to eye? — as it explores the effects of class, race, and heartrending star-crossed love in a story that's as provocative as it is powerful.

"Therese Anne Fowler has taken the ingredients of racism, justice, and conservative religion and has concocted a feast of a read: compelling, heartbreaking, and inevitable. I finished A Good Neighborhood *in a single sitting. Yes, it's that good."* —**Jodi Picoult**, #1 *New York Times* bestselling author of *Small Great Things* and *A Spark of Light*

"Compelling and captivating, A Good Neighborhood *left me speechless yet wanting to discuss. This is a story that will stick with you for a long time."* —**Emily Giffin**, #1 *New York Times* bestselling author of *All We Ever Wanted*

ABOUT THE AUTHOR: **Therese Anne Fowler** is the author of the *New York Times* bestselling novel *Z: A Novel of Zelda Fitzgerald* and *A Well-Behaved Woman*. Raised in the Midwest, she moved to North Carolina in 1995. She holds a BA in sociology/cultural anthropology and an MFA in creative writing from North Carolina State University.

February 2020 | Hardcover | $27.99 | 9781250237279 | St. Martin's Press

CONVERSATION STARTERS

1. Early in the novel, Juniper considers: "What, she wondered, made a neighborhood good? To her parents, good seemed to mean there were mainly other people like themselves." (50) What do you think makes a "good" neighborhood, and is Oak Knoll one of them? As new houses are built in older, existing neighborhoods, do you think that changes the feel and culture of a place?

2. Do you view the Whitman family as genuinely Christian, or is religion primarily a tool for Julia and Brad? Can both things be true at the same time?

3. Race can be a sensitive topic, and it features prominently in *A Good Neighborhood*. How comfortable do you feel talking about race, and do you think this novel changed your perspective on the role that race plays in the United States?

4. Almost immediately, we are told, "Later this summer when the funeral takes place, the media will speculate boldly on who's to blame. They'll challenge attendees to say on camera whose side they're on." (5) How does knowing that a tragedy lies ahead change your reading experience?

5. Who should shoulder the blame for the chain of aggression between these neighbors? What actions could have been taken by either family to tame the tension?

6. The Greek chorus makes the reader a part of the story, and complicit in the action. How did that affect your reading? Who did you believe the "we" was in the book's narration?

7. The book club in the novel is reading and discussing Vladimir Nabokov's *Lolita*. How does that classic novel echo or amplify the action in *A Good Neighborhood*?

8. "As our resident English professor would remind us, place, especially in stories of the South, is as much a character as any human, and inseparable from—in this case even necessary to—the plot." (13) The novel is set in North Carolina. How does the setting inform the story? Do you think that attitudes and ghosts of history impact the characters in the book?

THE GUEST BOOK
Sarah Blake

The thought-provoking new novel by *New York Times* bestselling author Sarah Blake

A lifetime of secrets. A history untold.

No. It is a simple word, uttered on a summer porch in 1936. And it will haunt Kitty Milton for the rest of her life. Kitty and her husband, Ogden, are both from families considered the backbone of the country. But this refusal will come to be Kitty's defining moment, and its consequences will ripple through the Milton family for generations. For while they summer on their island in Maine, anchored as they are to the way things have always been, the winds of change are beginning to stir.

In 1959 New York City, two strangers enter the Miltons' circle. One captures the attention of Kitty's daughter, while the other makes each of them question what the family stands for. This new generation insists the times are changing. And in one night, everything does.

So much so that in the present day, the third generation of Miltons doesn't have enough money to keep the island in Maine. Evie Milton's mother has just died, and as Evie digs into her mother's and grandparents' history, what she finds is a story as unsettling as it is inescapable, the story that threatens the foundation of the Milton family myth.

Moving through three generations and back and forth in time, The *Guest Book* asks how we remember and what we choose to forget. It shows the untold secrets we inherit and pass on, unknowingly echoing our parents and grandparents. Sarah Blake's triumphant novel tells the story of a family and a country that buries its past in quiet, until the present calls forth a reckoning.

"*Beautifully crafted ... The Milton family history, rife with secrets and moral failings, including a deep-seated bigotry, is a timely tale of America itself. An enveloping and moving page-turner.*" —***People*, Book of the Week**

ABOUT THE AUTHOR: **Sarah Blake** is the author of the novels *Grange House* and the *New York Times* bestseller *The Postmistress*. She lives in Washington, D.C., with her husband and two sons.

May 2019 | Hardcover | $27.99 | 9781250110251 | Flatiron Books

CONVERSATION STARTERS

1. Evie teaches her students that "history is sometimes made by heroes, but it is also always made by us. We, the people, who stumble around, who block or help the hero out of loyalty, stubbornness, faith, or fear. Those who wall up—and those who break through walls. The people at the edge of the photographs. The people watching—the crowd. You." Do you agree with her? How do the characters in this novel shape history? And whose history do they shape?

2. Central to Paul's academic work is the idea that "there is the crime and there is the silence." How does that statement echo throughout the novel, specifically in his and Evie's conversations about the stumble stones in Germany? What kinds of silences do we reproduce in our lives in this country now?

3. On the porch later that evening, after Kitty says no to Elsa, Kitty is maddened by Elsa's reading of her refusal. "For god's sake," she says, "it's not so simple." And Elsa replies, "But it is. It's very simple. It always is." Is Kitty's refusal simple? How might Neddy's death have shaped her thoughts? Does it let her off the hook in terms of Elsa's request?

4. Evie says of her parents' generation that they seem to have "inherited their days rather than chosen them, made do with what they had, and so they peopled the rooms rather than lived in them, ghosting their own lives." Is that a fair assessment? Discuss the similarities and differences between the various generations of Miltons in this novel in relation to what they have been given.

5. At Evelyn's engagement, Ogden toasts: "Behind every successful man is a good woman ... Or so the saying goes. But I suggest a good woman is the reason men put up walls and gardens, churches. The reason men build at all. At the center of every successful man is a good woman." Discuss the gender dynamics at play in the different marriages in this novel.

HOLLOW KINGDOM
Kira Jane Buxton

S.T., a domesticated crow, is a bird of simple pleasures: hanging out with his owner Big Jim, trading insults with Seattle's wild crows (those idiots), and enjoying the finest food humankind has to offer: Cheetos®.

Then Big Jim's eyeball falls out of his head, and S.T. starts to feel like something isn't quite right. His most tried-and-true remedies—from beak-delivered beer to the slobbering affection of Big Jim's loyal but dim-witted dog, Dennis—fail to cure Big Jim's debilitating malady. S.T. is left with no choice but to abandon his old life and venture out into a wild and frightening new world with his trusty steed Dennis, where he discovers that the neighbors are devouring each other and the local wildlife is abuzz with rumors of dangerous new predators roaming Seattle. Humanity's extinction has seemingly arrived, and the only one determined to save it is a foul-mouthed crow whose knowledge of the world around him comes from his TV-watching education.

Hollow Kingdom is a humorous, big-hearted, and boundlessly beautiful romp through the apocalypse and the world that comes after, where even a cowardly crow can become a hero.

"Hollow Kingdom *enriches our human experience by inhabiting the minds (and bellies!) of our non-human animal companions and reminding us that we're not alone here on this earth.*" —**Ruth Ozeki, author of** *A Tale for the Time Being*

"*What starts as a hilarious take on a zombie-like apocalypse as seen from the animal world becomes a compelling ecological tale. And S.T.'s emotional journey rivals any novel I've ever read.*" —**Laura Cummings, White Birch Books (North Conway, NH)**

ABOUT THE AUTHOR: **Kira Jane Buxton**'s writing has appeared in the *New York Times*, NewYorker.com, McSweeney's, *The Rumpus*, *Huffington Post*, and more. She calls the tropical utopia of Seattle, Washington, home and spends her time with three cats, a dog, two crows, a charm of hummingbirds, and a husband.

August 2019 | Hardcover | $27.00 | 9781538745823 | Grand Central Publishing

CONVERSATION STARTERS

1. In what ways is S.T. caught between the MoFo world and the world of nature? How does this affect his sense of self? How does it both benefit and impair him at various points in the novel?

2. S.T.'s relationship with Dennis evolves from S.T.'s deprecation and occasional hostility to a pure and loving friendship. In what ways do the unlikely duo complement each other? What do you think their bond stems from?

3. What other unlikely symbiotic relationships exist in the novel? What about in the real world?

4. Kraai initially claims that S.T. is "caged and clipped," an idea that S.T. angrily rejects. However, S.T. later loses his ability to fly due to a wing injury. How is this significant to S.T.'s character and place in the world?

5. Consider the way the natural world communicates and how rumors spread in this novel. How are *Aura*, *Echo*, and *Web* similar and different to methods of human communication?

6. Although he is absent for most of the story, Big Jim is periodically portrayed through flashbacks. How does his character develop and evolve through S.T.'s memories? How does your perception of Big Jim change throughout the novel?

7. S.T. often wonders at the ingenuity of humans, from inventions like Cheetos® and hot dog–eating competitions to "how even though MoFos weren't born with wings, they made their own and put them on airplanes and maxi pads, and [...] how they flushed all their poops out to *Echo*" (chapter 37). How does this reverence compare to his feelings for the natural world? Can you think of moments where S.T. displays the same awe for nature?

8. Besides Cheetos®, what do you think are the best inventions and characteristics of humanity? Of nature?

9. Why do you think the book is titled *Hollow Kingdom*?

10. Who is your favorite character? Why?

HOPE RIDES AGAIN: AN OBAMA BIDEN MYSTERY
Andrew Shaffer

Obama and Biden reprise their roles as BFFs—turned-detectives as they chase Obama's stolen cell phone through the streets of Chicago—and right into a vast conspiracy.

Following a long but successful book tour, Joe Biden has one more stop before he can return home: Chicago. His old pal Barack Obama has invited him to meet a wealthy benefactor whose endorsement could turn the tide for Joe if he decides to run for president.

The two friends barely have time to catch up before another mystery lands in their laps: Obama's prized Blackberry is stolen. When their number-one suspect winds up full of lead on the South Side, the police are content to write it off as just another gangland shooting. But Joe and Obama smell a rat ...

Set against the backdrop of a raucous city on St. Patrick's Day, Joe and Obama race to find the shooter, only to uncover a vast conspiracy that goes deeper than the waters of Lake Michigan—which is exactly where they'll spend the rest of their retirement if they're not careful.

"The game is afoot for Joe and Barry. This is fun, escapist fiction with enough details ...t o stay grounded in a kind of reality." —Booklist

"Once again, Shaffer convincingly portrays his unusual leads as action heroes." —Publishers Weekly

"It's a giddy premise, a bit of Resistance wish-fulfillment for those who'd like to see Biden and Obama trading one-liners and cracking skulls." —New Yorker on Hope Never Dies

ABOUT THE AUTHOR: **Andrew Shaffer** is the *New York Times* best-selling author of more than a dozen books, including the national best seller *Hope Never Dies: An Obama Biden Mystery*. He lives with his wife, the novelist Tiffany Reisz, in Kentucky.

July 2019 | Paperback | $14.99 | 9781683691228 | Quirk Books

CONVERSATION STARTERS

1. Why do you think that the fondness for Barack Obama and Joe Biden's "bromance" has persisted after their tenure in office?

2. Do you feel that Obama and Biden's voices were authentic to the men themselves? Why or why not?

3. What moments made you laugh?

4. What crime fighting duos from literature and pop culture do you think Obama and Biden best emulate?

5. Why do you think the author chose Chicago's gun violence crisis as the framing for this mystery?

6. What can our government officials learn from Obama and Biden's friendship?

7. Did you feel that this book was an escape from the current political climate?

8. Do you think that seeing elected officials portrayed as larger-than-life heroes could inspire readers to get more involved in politics?

9. What other political pairs would you like to see team up to solve a mystery?

10. There are quite a few famous cameos in *Hope Rides Again*. Which one was your favorite and why?

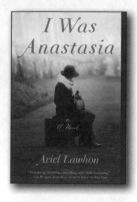

I WAS ANASTASIA
Ariel Lawhon

An enthralling feat of historical suspense that unravels the extraordinary twists and turns in Anna Anderson's fifty-year battle to be recognized as Anastasia Romanov. Is she the Russian Grand Duchess or the thief of another woman's legacy? Countless others have rendered their verdict. Now it is your turn. The question of who Anna Anderson is and what actually happened to Anastasia Romanov spans fifty years and touches three continents. This thrilling saga is every bit as moving and momentous as it is harrowing and twisted.

"Compelling and utterly fascinating." —Lisa Wingate, author of *Before We Were Yours*

"The fate of the Grand Duchess Anastasia, youngest daughter of the last Tsar, is an old mystery that never gets old. In the hands of Ariel Lawhon, it springs to life again, challenging everything we believe about what we remember and who we are. Was Anna Anderson really the only survivor of the Romanovs or was she a persistent fraud? Somehow, Lawhon, a masterly writer, not only leads her readers to ponder this riddle, but to care about it as well. This is a deft and deeply moving saga." —Jacquelyn Mitchard, *New York Times* bestselling author of *The Deep End of the Ocean*

ABOUT THE AUTHOR: **Ariel Lawhon** is cofounder of the popular website SheReads.org. A novelist, blogger, and lifelong reader, she lives in the rolling hills outside Nashville, Tennessee, with her husband, four sons, and black lab.

February 2019 | Paperback | $16.00 | 9781101973318 | Anchor

CONVERSATION STARTERS

1. *I Was Anastasia* is an unusually structured novel that moves backward and forward in time. Why do you think the author chose to tell the story in this way?

2. When we first meet Anna Anderson, she is not an easy character to like. As you learned more about her past, did your opinion of her change?

3. How do you interpret Anna's hoarding tendencies, especially with regard to animals?

4. Anna's story is told in the third person; Anastasia's story in the first person. What are your thoughts on the different points of view? Which did you prefer?

5. People often think of Anastasia Romanov in terms of the 1997 animated film. Yet this book does not portray her as a typical Disney princess. Were you glad to see a different side to this historic figure? Or did it bother you?

6. The bombing of Hannover (October 8, 1943) is a dramatic and terrifying scene in the book. Do you think you could display the same level of resilience if you were in Anna's shoes?

7. The longer the Romanovs were in captivity, the smaller their world became, until they were confined to a handful of rooms. They each handled the boredom and oppression differently. What would you have done in their situation?

8. Do your thoughts about Anna's identity shift as the novel progresses? Does she become more (or less) believable as we travel back in time with her?

9. Did reading this novel inspire you to find out more about the Romanovs?

10. The Romanovs are not the only royal family to come to a tragic end, yet their story endures as few have. What do you think contributes to the timeless fascination—that of Anastasia in particular?

11. Discuss the ending of the novel. How did it affect your feelings about the novel as a whole?

12. Did the Author's Note change your opinion about the ending?

IN THE NIGHT OF MEMORY
Linda LeGarde Grover

When Loretta surrenders her young girls to the county and then disappears, she becomes one more missing Native woman in Indian Country's long devastating history of loss. But she is also a daughter of the Mozhay Point Reservation in northern Minnesota and the mother of Azure and Rain, ages three and four, and her absence haunts all the lives she has touched—and all the stories they tell in this novel. Nuanced and moving, *In the Night of Memory* returns to the fictional reservation of Linda LeGarde Grover's previous award-winning books, introducing readers to a new generation of the Gallette family as Azure and Rain make their way home to their extended Mozhay family.

"In the Night of Memory *is character driven and lyrical. Its vast, distinct chorus of matrilineal American Indian voices ring in melancholic yet dauntless tones, clarifying that community and nurturing can ameliorate absence."* —*Foreword Reviews* (starred review)

"*Told with vibrancy by an Ojibwe professor and poet, this own voices story of Ojibwe girls in a situation only too common for indigenous families shouldn't be missed."* —*Library Journal*

"*With gorgeous imagery and verdant prose, LeGarde Grover's novel lays bare the pain and loss of indigenous women and children while simultaneously offering a ray of hope."* —*Publishers Weekly*

"*Grover creates a tapestry of history and imagination, a weaving of perspectives beautiful and wise, a collection of truths that anchors and honors the experiences of Indigenous women."* —**Kao Kalia Yang, author of** *The Song Poet: A Memoir of My Father*

"*Riding on the wave of this poignant novel are some of the most important issues affecting American Indians today. A remarkable achievement."* —**David Treuer, author of** *The Heartbeat of Wounded Knee*

ABOUT THE AUTHOR: **Linda LeGarde Grover** is professor of American Indian studies at the University of Minnesota Duluth and a member of the Bois Forte Band of Ojibwe. She is the award-winning author of *The Dance Boots*, *The Road Back to Sweetgrass*, *The Sky Watched*, and *Onigamiising*.

April 2019 | Hardcover | $22.95 | 9781517906504 | University of Minnesota Press

CONVERSATION STARTERS

1. Azure Gallette bases the memory of her mother Lorraine on one incident from her childhood, which may or not be true or accurate. Do you have a childhood memory that you have found to be embellished by imagination and memory or not true?

2. What events and situations in Loretta's and her family's history might have led to her losing her children?

3. A brother, invisible to everyone except Azure, appeared when she moved from a foster home into an institutional children's home. What might be some reasons for his appearance? Have you or someone you know ever had an imaginary friend?

4. What might be some of the reasons that led people to become foster parents to Azure and Rain?

5. Rainy's disabilities were not diagnosed until she was an adult; one result of this was that she didn't graduate from high school. Have you ever known or heard about a student with an undiagnosed learning/social condition?

6. There are so many reasons people fall in love! What made Loretta fall in love with Junior; what caused Azure to fall in love with Freddy? Is the old saying that love is blind sometimes true, wholly or partially?

7. Boyhood friends Junior and Howard both went to Vietnam and remained friends afterwards, yet their lives after they returned differed in many ways. What might be some of the factors in the differences? Have you known someone who was a soldier in Vietnam?

8. In this story, older women recount much of the history of Azure and Rainy's extended family and circle of acquaintances; the older women also explain their views on the histories and reasons behind events. There is no clear identification of these women as feminists—but in what ways might that term fit?

9. There is no "happily ever after" in this novel, yet Azure, by middle age, expresses an acceptance and contentment with her life—would this equate to happiness, and how necessary do you feel happiness is to a good life?

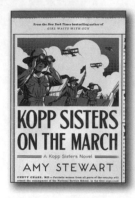

KOPP SISTERS ON THE MARCH: A KOPP SISTERS NOVEL

Amy Stewart

All four previous books in the Kopp Sisters series have been Indie Next Picks.

In the fifth installment of Amy Stewart's clever and original Kopp Sisters series, the sisters learn some military discipline—whether they're ready or not—as the U.S. prepares to enter World War I.

In *Kopp Sisters on the March*, the women of Camp Chevy Chase face down the skepticism of the War Department, the double standards of a scornful public, and the very real perils of war. Once again, Amy Stewart has brilliantly brought a little-known moment in history to light with her fearless and funny Kopp sisters novels.

"Told in Stewart's nimble, witty prose, this fifth in the popular series is based largely on fact and offers a paean to patriotism and the role women have played in war, even a century ago. Devoted fans will be pleased with the tantalizing hint Stewart provides about what lies ahead for Constance."
—*Booklist*, **starred review**

ABOUT THE AUTHOR: **Amy Stewart** is the *New York Times* best-selling author of the acclaimed Kopp Sisters series, which began with *Girl Waits with Gun*. Her six nonfiction books include *The Drunken Botanist* and *Wicked Plants*. She and her husband own a bookstore called Eureka Books. She lives in Portland, Oregon.

September 2019 | Hardcover | $26.00 | 9781328736529 | HMH Books

CONVERSATION STARTERS

1. Constance is still having trouble adjusting to her more domestic life. She even looks for her whistle to direct traffic on their way into camp on page 15. Norma notices and says, "Go ahead and order them out of the way. You like to be in charge." How did it feel seeing Constance's listlessness here compared to the previous books?

2. On page 28 Constance describes the scene at the school: "The place had the air of a summer party, in spite of the early March chill, and seemed far removed from the fighting in France or, for that matter, the very idea of war." The disconnection between the camp and the war is brought up many times throughout the book. Why does it seem so far removed? Does that change during the course of the story?

3. "There are times when I find the law to be more of a hindrance." (293) Usually Constance is teaching others, but what does Nurse Cartwright teach Constance?

4. What do you think about Norma's point: "If the only woman in Congress votes for war, every mother in this country will give up her son a little more easily"? How can a woman's public decision be helpful or hurtful differently than a man's?

5. "It's my camp. We're going to train for war." (323) This change in Constance's behavior is where we see the character most like the Constance we have seen in previous books. What sparked this change the most? Where does her confidence come from?

6. On page 337 Maude Miner says, "I've never been prouder of this country's daughters than I am right now." Why was it so important for her to see the women's training in person even if at first she thought it was a detriment to their cause? What did it show her personally and what does she hope it will show men?

7. A time when family are scattered and not a text or Facebook message away, how does that impact the choices the family members who are "left behind" make?

8. The epilogue is set six months later and only focuses on Beulah and Nurse Cartwright. What did you think about this ending?

THE LAKE ON FIRE
Rosellen Brown

The Lake on Fire is an epic narrative that begins among 19th century Jewish immigrants on a failing Wisconsin farm. Dazzled by lore of the American dream, Chaya and her strange, brilliant, younger brother Asher stow away to Chicago. What they discover there, however, is a Gilded Age as empty a façade as the beautiful Columbian Exposition luring thousands to Lake Michigan's shore. The pair scrapes together a meager living—Chaya in a cigar factory; Asher, roaming the city and stealing books and jewelry to share with the poor—until each finds a different path of escape. An examination of family, love, and revolution, this profound tale resonates eerily with today's current events and tumultuous social landscape. *The Lake on Fire* is robust, gleaming, and gritty all at once, proving that celebrated author Rosellen Brown is back with a story as luminous as ever.

*"... stellar, evocative ..." —**Publishers Weekly***

*"A transporting drama of class and love, steeped in period feeling, written with beauty and conviction." —**Kirkus Reviews***

*"Brown imaginatively, compassionately, and spellbindingly dramatizes timeless questions of survival and social conscience." —**Booklist***

*"Rosellen Brown has a great ear, a great eye, a great love of the painful twists and turns that happen in a human life and the big twists and turns of American history." —**The New York Times***

*"If you don't know this name, get familiar: Brown is one of our best living fiction writers." —**Entertainment Weekly***

ABOUT THE AUTHOR: **Rosellen Brown** is the author of the novels *Civil Wars*, *Half a Heart*, *Tender Mercies*, *Before and After*, and six other books. Her stories have appeared frequently in *O. Henry Prize Stories*, *Best American Short Stories* and *Best Short Stories of the Century*. She now teaches in the MFA in Writing Program at the School of the Art Institute of Chicago and lives in Mr. Obama's neighborhood, overlooking Lake Michigan.

October 2018 | Paperback | $17.95 | 9781946448231 | Sarabande Books

CONVERSATION STARTERS

1. What is the role of literature for the characters of *The Lake on Fire*, and what does the book envision as the role of literature in society? How does the book question the value of literature in times of inequality and social unrest, and how does the book affirm the value of literature?

2. How does loss shape Chaya's and Asher's experiences?

3. Discuss the role of religion in Chaya and Asher's view of the world. How does it affect the ways in which the world views them?

4. In what ways does the book show the effects of capitalism on the body of workers? How are the bodies of men and women treated differently? How are bodies treated differently on the farm versus in the factory?

5. What does Ms. Gottlieb mean by "principles cost money"? Do you agree? Are principles a privilege? If this is true, does it invalidate principles? Does it excuse unprincipled acts? Who in the book compromises their principles and who refuses to? What effects do these compromises or non-compromises have on the people around them?

6. Chaya makes multiple attempts to return to places and people she has left. Is she successful? What would a successful return look like for her?

7. Consider the significance of the World's Fair in the novel. How is it used as a setting to explore progress, inequality, and the relationship between the two?

8. How are fairy tales used to explore the themes of the novel? How are they subverted?

THE LAST BOOK PARTY

Karen Dukess

A propulsive tale of ambition and romance, set in the publishing world of 1980's New York and the timeless beaches of Cape Cod.

In the summer of 1987, 25-year-old Eve Rosen is an aspiring writer languishing in a low-level assistant job. With her professional ambitions floundering, Eve jumps at the chance to attend an early summer gathering at the Cape Cod home of famed New Yorker writer Henry Grey and his poet wife, Tillie.

Dazzled by the guests and her burgeoning crush on the hosts' son, Eve lands a new job as Henry Grey's research assistant and an invitation to Henry and Tillie's exclusive and famed "Book Party"—where attendees dress as literary characters. But by the night of the party, Eve discovers uncomfortable truths about her summer entanglements and understands that the literary world she so desperately wanted to be a part of is not at all what it seems.

A page-turning, coming-of-age story, written with a lyrical sense of place and a profound appreciation for the sustaining power of books, Karen Dukess's *The Last Book Party* shows what happens when youth and experience collide and what it takes to find your own voice.

ABOUT THE AUTHOR: With a background in newspaper and magazine journalism, **Karen Dukess** spent nearly a decade as a speechwriter on gender equality at the United Nations Development Programme. She is a graduate of Brown University and the Columbia University Graduate School of Journalism and lives in Pelham, New York. *The Last Book Party* is her debut novel.

July 2019 | Hardcover | $27.00 | 9781250225474 | Henry Holt & Company

CONVERSATION STARTERS

1. *The Last Book Party* is the title but it is only a small part of the book. Why do you think the book party is so important to Eve and the other characters?

2. On page 16 Alva tells Eve to re-read *I Capture the Castle*. What was she trying to communicate to Eve by recommending it?

3. Place is a large part of this book. Why do you think the Cape is so soothing for Eve? What do you notice about the way she thinks about Florida versus the Cape?

4. Eve seems a bit naïve to the relationships and identities of many characters, but she very clearly defines the roles at the publishing house. Why do you think she can see these roles so clearly, but she has a harder time outside of work?

5. Eve is treated without as much respect because she is female. Do you think the way she is treated is specific to 1987 or do you think these issues are still present today?

6. What other differences and similarities do you see between 1987 in the novel and today in terms of gender, career, relationships, and social values?

7. Eve's relationship with Danny seems to be another example of her feeling less important. Do you think this has to do with his career or with their gender? Do you think their parents would have handled the depression differently if it had been Eve instead of Danny?

8. Why do you think Eve is so suspicious immediately of Jeremy when she is otherwise so non-judgmental of other characters?

9. Jeremy challenges Eve's idea of being a writer and how to write. He sees it as hard work and not as a gift. Why do you think Eve created this idea of being a writer? Why does she seem surprised by Jeremy's feelings on the topic?

10. In some ways Eve seems much younger than 25 years old. How do you think Alva and Malcolm and her parents are trying to help or hinder her growth?

MILKMAN
Anna Burns

Winner of the 2018 Man Booker Prize

A *New York Times* Best Seller

In an unnamed city, middle sister stands out for the wrong reasons. She reads while walking, for one. And she has been taking French night classes downtown. So when a local paramilitary known as the milkman begins pursuing her, she suddenly becomes "interesting," the last thing she ever wanted to be. Despite middle sister's attempts to avoid him—and to keep her mother from finding out about her maybe-boyfriend—rumors spread and the threat of violence lingers. *Milkman* is a story of the way inaction can have enormous repercussions, in a time when the wrong flag, wrong religion, or even a sunset can be subversive. Told with ferocious energy and sly, wicked humor, *Milkman* establishes Anna Burns as one of the most consequential voices of our day.

"*Bursting with energy, with tiny apertures of kindness, and a youthful kind of joy ... A triumph of resistance.*" —**The Boston Globe**

"*Seething with black humor and adolescent anger at the adult world and its brutal absurdities ... For a novel about life under multifarious forms of totalitarian control—political, gendered, sectarian, communal—*Milkman *can be charmingly wry.*" —**The New Yorker**

"Milkman *vibrates with the anxieties of our own era, from terrorism to sexual harassment to the blinding divisions that make reconciliation feel impossible ... It's as though the intense pressure of this place has compressed the elements of comedy and horror to produce some new alloy.*" —**The Washington Post**

ABOUT THE AUTHOR: **Anna Burns** was born in Belfast, Northern Ireland. She is the author of two other novels, *No Bones* and *Little Constructions* (coming from Graywolf Press in February 2020), and of the novella *Mostly Hero*. She lives in East Sussex, England.

December 2018 | Paperback | $16.00 | 9781644450000 | Graywolf Press

CONVERSATION STARTERS

1. When and where does *Milkman* take place? How do you know?

2. How did the author's avoidance of proper names, for both people and places, affect your experience of reading the book?

3. How do various characters in the novel express their political allegiances?

4. The milkman causes extreme fear and anxiety for middle sister, complicating her life even though their interactions are quite brief and never physical. Where does this power come from? Is it violent?

5. How does the milkman compare to villains you have encountered in other stories?

6. Even before the rumors about the milkman, middle sister aroused suspicions due to her unusual tendency to read while walking. What are some of the other reasons people in the community have come to be considered "beyond the pale"? How are these designations decided and enforced? Are there exceptions?

7. How is the "real milkman" significant to middle sister, to her family, and to the novel?

8. Complex feelings lie just below the surface in middle sister's family, particularly between her and her mother. How does their relationship change during the course of the novel?

9. Who is middle sister closest to? Who does she turn to when she needs to talk?

10. What are some cultural similarities or differences between the community in *Milkman* and your own?

MIDNIGHT AT THE BLACKBIRD CAFÉ
Heather Webber

Nestled in the mountain shadows of Alabama lies the little town of Wicklow. It is here that Anna Kate has returned to bury her beloved Granny Zee, owner of the Blackbird Café.

It was supposed to be a quick trip to close the café and settle her grandmother's estate, but despite her best intentions to avoid forming ties or even getting to know her father's side of the family, Anna Kate finds herself inexplicably drawn to the quirky Southern town her mother ran away from so many years ago, and the mysterious blackbird pie everybody can't stop talking about.

As the truth about her past slowly becomes clear, Anna Kate will need to decide if this lone blackbird will finally be able to take her broken wings and fly.

"*Midnight at the Blackbird Café is an enchanting gem of a novel, brimming with charming characters, heartwarming connections, old secrets, and a southern setting that makes you want to move there. As refreshing as a glass of blackberry tea, this is truly magical realism at its best!*" —**Karen White, New York Times bestselling author**

"*A tantalizing, delicious delight, through and through. Heather Webber writes with so much detail and imagination that I'll be craving some Blackbird Café pie—and the comfort that comes with it—for a long time to come.*" —**Kristin Harmel, international bestselling author of The Room on Rue Amélie**

ABOUT THE AUTHOR: **Heather Webber** is the author of more than twenty mystery novels, including the Nina Quinn series, and has been twice nominated for an Agatha Award. She's a homebody who loves to be close to her family, read, watch reality TV (especially cooking competition shows), drink too much coffee, crochet, and bake (mostly cookies). Heather grew up in a suburb of Boston, but currently she lives in the Cincinnati area with her family and is hard at work on her next book.

July 2019 | Hardcover | $24.99 | 9781250198594 | Forge Books
January 2020 | Paperback | $17.99 | 9781250198617 | Forge Books

CONVERSATION STARTERS

1. As this story begins, Anna Kate has put her life on hold to move to Wicklow, Alabama. She's been uprooted from everything familiar and has settled in a small, two-stoplight town where she knows no one. Though she initially has regrets about the move, she is determined to stay put. Have you ever been in a similar situation? If so, how did you adjust to your new surroundings?

2. Anna Kate comes to recognize that she's been heavily influenced by her mother's memories of the Lindens. When it becomes clear that Eden's recollections may not tell the whole story, Anna Kate sets out to form her own opinions about her father's side of the family. Have you ever been influenced by someone only to realize that person was wrong? How did you correct the situation?

3. Anna Kate goes out of her way to help Summer secure college funds by selling T-shirts and Summer's father's blackberry tea, and also helps them ready their property to use as a B&B. Why do you think Anna Kate was compelled to help this young woman she barely knew?

4. Mr. Lazenby regularly eats a piece of blackbird pie in order to connect with his dearly-departed wife, but Faylene decided to stop eating the pie in order to move on from the loss of her husband. If you could eat a piece of blackbird pie to communicate with a deceased loved one, would you? Why or why not?

5. Anna Kate made a promise to her mother and ultimately broke it. Do you agree with Natalie that some promises are made to be broken? Have you ever broken a promise? How did you feel afterward?

6. The author acknowledges this book was born from an obsession with the Beatles' song "Blackbird." The line "Take these broken wings and learn to fly" shaped nearly every character in different ways. How do you think this lyric relates to Anna Kate, Natalie, Seelie, Summer, and Aubin? How were they broken? How did they learn to fly?

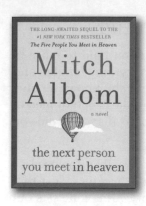

THE NEXT PERSON YOU MEET IN HEAVEN
Mitch Albom

In Mitch Albom's beloved novel, *The Five People You Meet in Heaven*, the world fell in love with Eddie, a grizzled war veteran- turned-amusement park mechanic who died saving the life of a young girl named Annie. Eddie's journey to heaven taught him that every life matters. Now, in this magical sequel, Mitch Albom reveals Annie's story.

The accident that killed Eddie left an indelible mark on Annie. It took her left hand, which needed to be surgically reattached. Injured, scarred, and unable to remember why, Annie's life is forever changed by a guilt-ravaged mother who whisks her away from the world she knew. Bullied by her peers and haunted by something she cannot recall, Annie struggles to find acceptance as she grows. When, as a young woman, she reconnects with Paulo, her childhood love, she believes she has finally found happiness.

As the novel opens, Annie is marrying Paulo. But when her wedding day ends in an unimaginable accident, Annie finds herself on her own heavenly journey—and an inevitable reunion with Eddie, one of the five people who will show her how her life mattered in ways she could not have fathomed.

ABOUT THE AUTHOR: **Mitch Albom** is a best-selling author, screenwriter, playwright and nationally-syndicated columnist. The author of five consecutive #1 *New York Times* bestsellers, his books have collectively sold more than 33 million copies in forty-two languages worldwide. *Tuesdays With Morrie*, which spent four straight years atop the *New York Times* list, is now the bestselling memoir of all time. Four of Albom's books, including Morrie, *The Five People You Meet In Heaven*, *For One More Day* and *Have A Little Faith*, have been made into highly acclaimed TV movies. He has founded six charities in and around Detroit, including the first ever 24-hour medical clinic for homeless children in America, and also operates an orphanage in Port-Au-Prince, Haiti. Albom lives with his wife, Janine, in metropolitan Detroit.

October 2019 | Paperback | $15.99 | 9780062294456 | Harper Paperbacks

CONVERSATION STARTERS

1. Why are endings often so difficult and challenging? What's a healthy balance between staying connected and moving on?

2. What does Annie understand as a nurse that many people may not?

3. Central to Annie's story and her feelings about herself are supposed mistakes. What constitutes a mistake? In what contexts or situations are they allowable or even necessary?

4. What is Annie's distant connection to Sameer? How is it that we can be connected to people we have never met? Who might you be distantly connected to?

5. Sameer "chose to flip [his] human existence" and confront the thing he feared most. What stops many people from doing this while alive?

6. Throughout the story, vibrant colors are described. What do such details add? Why are they important to the subject?

7. Consider Annie's mother, Lorraine. In what ways was she a good mother or not? What influence did Annie's father have on the two of them?

8. How is it that Cleo, a dog, can be one of the most important "people" in Annie's life? What makes dogs such good potential companions for humans? What are the limitations to the powerful relationships with a pet?

9. What is the potential value of loneliness? What determines when it becomes debilitating or dangerous?

10. Paulo believes Annie's injury makes her unique in a valuable way, while she laments being so different. What's the difference between different or unique? Why is difference in others so often shunned, while most people seem to want to be individuals themselves?

11. Lorraine tries to teach Annie about the danger of keeping secrets: "We think by keeping them, we're controlling things, but all the while, they're controlling us." What does she mean? How is it that secrets can be unhealthy? Are held secrets helpful?

12. Annie was named after a courageous woman who, at age 63, went over Niagara Falls in a barrel. What is courage? How is it different from bravery or recklessness?

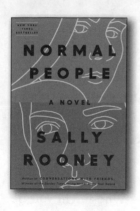

NORMAL PEOPLE
Sally Rooney

New York Times Best Seller

Longlisted for the Man Booker Prize

Coming to Hulu in 2020

At school Connell and Marianne pretend not to know each other. He's popular and well-adjusted, star of the school football team, while she is lonely, proud, and intensely private. But when Connell comes to pick his mother up from her job at Marianne's house, a strange and indelible connection grows between the two teenagers—one they are determined to conceal.

A year later, they're both studying at Trinity College in Dublin. Marianne has found her feet in a new social world while Connell hangs at the sidelines, shy and uncertain. Throughout their years at university, Marianne and Connell circle one another, straying toward other people and possibilities but always magnetically, irresistibly drawn back together. And as she veers into self-destruction and he begins to search for meaning elsewhere, each must confront how far they are willing to go to save the other.

Sally Rooney brings her brilliant psychological acuity and perfectly spare prose to a story that explores the subtleties of class, the electricity of first love, and the complex entanglements of family and friendship.

"A stunning novel about the transformative power of relationships" —**People**

"A master of the literary page-turner" —**J. Courtney Sullivan**

"Fresh and accessible ... There is so much to say about Rooney's fiction—in my experience, when people who've read her meet they tend to peel off into corners to talk." —**Dwight Garner,** *The New York Times*

ABOUT THE AUTHOR: **Sally Rooney** was born in the west of Ireland in 1991. Her work has appeared in *The New Yorker*, *The New York Times*, *Granta* and *The London Review of Books*. Winner of the *Sunday Times* Young Writer of the Year Award in 2017, she is the author of *Conversations with Friends* and the editor of the Irish literary journal *The Stinging Fly*.

April 2019 | Hardcover | $26.00 | 9781984822178 | Hogarth

....

CONVERSATION STARTERS

1. While living at home in Carricklea, Connell's sense of self is managed by the opinions of his peers in secondary school. To that end, he avoids being publicly seen with Marianne, an outcast in school, fearing how their association might damage his reputation. Were you critical of Connell for the way he treated Marianne in school, or were you sympathetic toward his adolescent self-consciousness? Do you think he became less concerned by the thoughts of others as he grew older?

2. With Marianne, Connell feels a sense of "total privacy" in which "he could tell her anything about himself, even weird things, and she would never repeat them, he knows that. Being alone with her is like opening a door away from normal life and then closing it behind him." (6–7) Why do you think Connell is sometimes unnerved by their intense and intimate connection? Further, why do you think he's unsettled by the sense that Marianne would do anything to please him?

3. The first time Connell tells Marianne he loves her, we are told that "She has never believed herself fit to be loved by any person. But now she has a new life, of which this is the first moment, and even after many years have passed she will still think: Yes, that was it, the beginning of my life." (46) Do you think Marianne had ever been told that she was loved, in any sense of the word, by anyone before Connell? How can the experience of "first love" transform a person's self-image and view of the world?

4. In *Normal People*, Marianne only barely opens up to Connell about her relationship with her family—how her father had been violent when he was alive, how her brother verbally and physically attacks her, and how her mother essentially forbids her to believe that she is "special" in any way. How does Marianne's family influence her opinion of herself and affect her relationships with other people? How does she attempt to distance herself from her family? And how does Connell's upbringing compare and contrast to Marianne's?

5. How would you describe the power that Connell and Marianne hold over each other? Did you notice a power relation shift and evolve between them over the years? How might it have had both positive and negative effects in different moments?

142 OSTRICHES
April Dávila

Part love letter to the California desert, part intimate portrait of a family reckoning with drug abuse and denial, April Dávila's beautifully written debut captures the anxieties of a young woman who suddenly bears responsibility amid great stress ...

When Tallulah Jones was thirteen, her grandmother plucked her from the dank Oakland apartment she shared with her unreliable mom and brought her to the family ostrich ranch in the Mojave Desert. After eleven years caring for the curious, graceful birds, Tallulah accepts a job in Montana and prepares to leave home. But when Grandma Helen dies under strange circumstances, Tallulah inherits everything—just days before the birds inexplicably stop laying eggs.

Guarding the secret of the suddenly barren birds, Tallulah endeavors to force through a sale of the ranch, a task that is complicated by the arrival of her extended family. Their designs on the property, and deeply rooted dysfunction, threaten Tallulah's ambitions and eventually her life. With no options left, Tallulah must pull her head out of the sand and face the fifty-year legacy of a family in turmoil: the reality of her grandmother's death, her mother's alcoholism, her uncle's covetous anger, and the 142 ostriches whose lives are in her hands.

ABOUT THE AUTHOR: **April Dávila** is a fourth generation Californian and author. Her mother's family established a Sacramento Valley dairy farm in the 1880s and she has lived briefly in places as far flung as Ecuador, the Caribbean, and the Marshall Islands, but always comes back to California. She studied marine biology at Scripps College before going on to study writing at USC. An attendee of the Squaw Valley Community of Writers and past resident at the Dorland Mountain Arts Colony, she runs LitWeekLA, a weekly newsletter covering Los Angeles area literary events.

February 2020 | Paperback | $15.95 | 9781496724700 | Kensington Books

CONVERSATION STARTERS

1. Consider the role of men in this story. What kind of partner do you think Tallulah will end up with?

2. Why do you think the birds stop laying eggs?

3. Why is Tallulah so reluctant to share her inheritance?

4. How has substance abuse affected the Jones family?

5. Is Tallulah a good person?

6. In what ways is Sombra like other small towns? In what ways is it different?

7. How would the story be different if it were told from Uncle Steve's perspective? What about Aunt Christine's perspective?

8. One of the main themes of the story is motherhood. Consider how Tallulah's mom, Aunt Christine and Grandma Helen differ in their mothering styles. What are the repercussions of their parenting?

9. How would the story be different on another type of ranch? A cattle ranch? Chickens?

10. What's your opinion of Laura's whiskey glass theory?

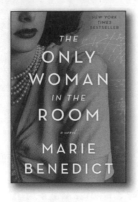

THE ONLY WOMAN IN THE ROOM
Marie Benedict

She possessed a stunning beauty. She also possessed a stunning mind. Could the world handle both?

Her beauty almost certainly saved her from the rising Nazi party and led to marriage with an Austrian arms dealer. Underestimated in everything else, she overheard the Third Reich's plans while at her husband's side, understanding more than anyone would guess. She devised a plan to flee in disguise from their castle, and the whirlwind escape landed her in Hollywood. She became Hedy Lamarr, screen star.

But she kept a secret more shocking than her heritage or her marriage: she was a scientist. And she knew a few secrets about the enemy. She had an idea that might help the country fight the Nazis ... if anyone would listen to her.

A powerful novel based on the incredible true story of the glamour icon and scientist whose groundbreaking invention revolutionized modern communication, *The Only Woman in the Room* is a masterpiece.

"A page-turning tapestry of intrigue and glamour. Spellbinding and timely." —**Fiona Davis, national bestselling author of** *The Masterpiece*

"Relevant today... a worthy read about this gorgeous and talented woman." —*New York Journal of Books*

"This. Book. Is. Amazing." —*Women's Day*

ABOUT THE AUTHOR: **Marie Benedict** is a lawyer with more than ten years' experience as a litigator at two of the country's premier law firms and for Fortune 500 companies. She is a magna cum laude graduate of Boston College with a focus in history and art history and a cum laude graduate of the Boston University School of Law. She is also the author of *The Other Einstein* and *Carnegie's Maid*. She lives in Pittsburgh with her family.

January 2019 | Hardcover | $25.99 | 9781492666868 | Sourcebooks Landmark
August 2019 | Paperback | $16.99 | 9781492666899 | Sourcebooks Landmark

CONVERSATION STARTERS

1. *The Only Woman in the Room* opens in Austria at a pivotal time in the years leading up to World War II. How familiar were you with the events of this era, particularly the European political developments and the relationship of Austria with Italy, Germany, and its other neighbors? Did you learn anything new about this period in history?

2. Did you find yourself becoming angry by Fritz's treatment of Hedy and her decision to stay in the marriage for so long? Would you have felt as bound to the promise to her father—that she will use Fritz as a shield and stay with him unless she has no other choice—as she did? How did this sense of duty motivate her decisions and actions at this stage? What did you think about her mother's views on the marital vow?

3. What are some of the differences between the life of Hedy the movie star and public figure and Hedy the scientist and private person? How does the theme of wearing masks appear throughout the novel? Do you feel this divide between women's exterior and interior lives exists today?

4. What was your reaction to learning that Hedy, an actress who was largely self-taught in the sciences, was responsible, in part, for an invention that ultimately formed the basis for cell-phone technology? Do you think our perceptions might still be unconsciously affected by lingering preconceptions from Hedy's day? How did her sense of duty and responsibility motivate her to create her invention?

5. The title of the novel is subject to several interpretations. What meanings can you glean from the title, and how did your understanding of the meaning of *The Only Woman in the Room* change from the beginning of the novel, to the end, if at all?

6. How might Hedy have symbolic importance in our time? Do you think it is important to uncover the voices and stories of historical women, and if so, why?

THE ORPHAN COLLECTOR
Ellen Marie Wiseman

With vivid writing and immediately absorbing characters, Ellen Marie Wiseman weaves a powerful tale of upheaval, resilience and hope amidst the tragic 1918 influenza—the pandemic that went on to infect one-third of the world's population ...

In the fall of 1918, thirteen-year-old German immigrant Pia Lange longs to be far from Philadelphia's overcrowded slums and the anti-immigrant sentiment that compelled her father to enlist in the U.S. Army. But as her city celebrates the end of war, an even more urgent threat arrives: the Spanish flu. Funeral crepe and quarantine signs appear on doors as victims drop dead in the streets and desperate survivors wear white masks to ward off illness. When food runs out in the cramped tenement she calls home, Pia must venture alone into the quarantined city in search of supplies, leaving her baby brothers behind.

Bernice Groves has become lost in grief and bitterness since her baby died from the Spanish flu. Watching Pia leave her brothers alone, Bernice makes a shocking, life-altering decision that leads her on a sinister mission to transform the city's orphans and immigrant children into what she feels are "true Americans."

Waking in a makeshift hospital days after collapsing in the street, Pia is frantic to return home. Instead, she is taken to St. Vincent's Orphan Asylum—the first step in a long and arduous journey to find her way back to her remaining family. As Bernice plots to keep the truth hidden at any cost in the months and years that follow, Pia must confront her own shame and fear, ultimately risking everything to see justice—and love—triumph at last.

ABOUT THE AUTHOR: **Ellen Marie Wiseman** is the bestselling author of highly acclaimed historical fiction novels, including *What She Left Behind* and *The Life She Was Given*, which was a Great Group Reads selection of the Women's National Book Association. She's a first-generation German American who discovered her love of reading and writing while attending first grade in one of the last one-room schoolhouses in New York State.

July 2020 | Paperback | $16.95 | 9781496715869 | Kensington Books

CONVERSATION STARTERS

1. No other pandemic has claimed as many lives as the influenza epidemic that swept the world in 1918-1919—not even the Black Death in the 14th century or AIDS in the 20th century—yet the Spanish Flu is seldom mentioned or even remembered. Why do you think that is? Did you know about the pandemic before reading *The Orphan Collector*?

2. Have you ever heard of or met anyone with Pia's ability to sense illness in others? Would you want to be able to tell when other people are sick before they know it themselves? Why or why not?

3. When Pia knocks on her neighbors' doors looking for food, no one will answer. Would you have answered the door if Pia knocked looking for food? What would you do if you were a poor immigrant in that situation?

4. During the time of the Spanish flu, people used all kinds of folk remedies to protect themselves from illness and help cure disease, many of which we now consider useless and even dangerous. Can you think of any other strange things people did in the past to cure or protect themselves from illness? Do you think there are folk or natural remedies that actually work?

5. Though the disease knew no gender, racial, or ethnic boundaries, Philadelphia's immigrant poor suffered the worst, with the largest loss of life happening in the slums and tenement districts. Why do you think that was? What issues do you think contributed to it?

6. Do you think Pia should feel so guilty about losing her brothers? Do you think it would have been helpful if she had told the nuns at St. Vincent's what happened? Should she have told Dr. and Mrs. Hudson sooner?

7. Disguised as a nurse, Bernice does a lot of horrible things to the immigrants in Philadelphia. What do you think is her worst crime? Do you think she paid for what she did?

8. How did you feel about Bernice when you first met her? When did your perception of her change? How and why did it change?

THE RED ADDRESS BOOK
Sofia Lundberg

A Publishers Lunch Buzz Book

A *Library Reads* Selection

An iBooks Most Anticipated Titles of 2019

A *West Virginia Gazette* "Books to Check out in the New Year" Pick

For fans of *The Little Paris Bookshop* and *The 100 Year-Old-Man Who Climbed Out the Window and Disappeared* comes a heartwarming debut about 96-year-old Doris, who writes down the memories of her eventful life as she pages through her decades-old address book. But the most profound moment of her life is still to come ...

The Red Address Book is a charming novel that prompts reflection on the stories we all should carry to the next generation, and the surprises in life that can await even the oldest among us, a debut novel that introduces Sofia Lundberg as a wise—and irresistible—storyteller.

"Written with love, told with joy. Very easy to enjoy." —**Fredrik Backman, author of** *A Man Called Ove*

"A sweet-tart Swedish romance steeped in memory and regret ... The Red Address Book *is just the sort of easy-reading tale that will inspire readers to pull up a comfy chair to the fire, grab a mug of cocoa and a box of tissues and get hygge with it."* —**Helen Simonson,** *New York Times Book Review*

"Wise and captivating, Lundberg's novel offers clear-eyed insights into old age and the solace of memory." —*People*

ABOUT THE AUTHOR: **Sofia Lundberg** is a journalist and former magazine editor. Her debut novel, *The Red Address Book*, was published in thirty-three territories worldwide. She lives in Stockholm with her son.

September 2019 | Paperback | $15.99 | 9780358108542 | HMH Books

CONVERSATION STARTERS

1. Why do you think Doris calls her red address book "a map of [her] life"? (7) Why does she want to tell her grandniece Jenny about it?

2. Look at Doris's childhood. Why does Doris's mother send her away as a child? What is Doris exposed to during this time that she had not previously known about or experienced before? What surprised you, or what did you learn, about this time period in Sweden?

3. Who is Gösta Nilsson and how does Doris meet him? Why do you think that Gösta and Doris are able to form such a close and enduring relationship?

4. Who stops Doris on the street on her way to the butcher and how does this encounter change her life? Is the encounter a lucky one or an unfortunate one? What does Doris say "might be one of the most degrading things you can subject someone to"? (50) Why does she put up with this degradation herself?

5. What does the book reveal about the subject of beauty? What does Doris learn about beauty during her time as a live mannequin? Why does she say that beauty is "the most manipulative force of all"? (78) Do you agree with her? Do Doris's ideas about beauty evolve as she ages?

6. Why does Doris say that separation is "the worst thing on earth?" (98) How is Doris's life shaped by the separations that occur? What other separations occur throughout the book and how do the characters cope with them?

7. What does the book seem to suggest about how well we can truly know others? How well did Jenny know her great aunt Doris? Were you surprised by any of the details from Doris's life? What secrets do she and other characters keep?

8. When Doris begins to write for a living, what does she instinctively know that people will want in their stories? Why do she and Gösta laugh at the stories she writes for women's magazines? What do you think the author is trying to convey about storytelling and its role in our lives?

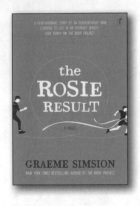

THE ROSIE RESULT
Graeme Simsion

In *The Rosie Project*, the first book in the trilogy, Don Tillman gives a lecture on Asperger's Syndrome. This sets up the premise that Don has autistic traits but doesn't recognize them in himself. By the end of *The Rosie Result*, though, both Don and his son Hudson identify as autistic.

If the storylines in *The Rosie Result* center on Don's challenges in trying to parent a son who shares many similarities with him, the novel's main theme is labeling and identity. The book directly questions many people's assumptions about autism. Questioning on this issue can be found throughout *The Rosie Result*, including in Don's thoughts. Should he and Rosie have Hudson assessed? What are the benefits and disadvantages of a diagnosis? Should autistic people have to adjust their behavior and thinking to match neurotypical norms? Does it make their lives better or worse if they do?

As Don ponders these questions, he is trying to be the best parent he can be. He remembers his own experiences as a child and an adult, and wonders what would have made things better for him. He starts thinking about his father, understanding and valuing some of what his father did for him, but also trying to come up with a new and better way to be a parent to Hudson. Don realizes that Hudson is similar to him, but not the same.

"Fiction as good as it gets, truly taking you into another world—and laugh-out-loud funny as well." —**Nicholas Kristof's** *New York Times* **newsletter**

"Just the right balance between serious literary exploration of social issues and ... delightfully humorous (mis)adventures." —*New York Journal of Books*

"Simsion's message of inclusiveness and embracing differences is lovely." —**NPR.org**

"Charming, eloquent, and insightful." —*Booklist* **(starred review)**

ABOUT THE AUTHOR: **Graeme Simsion** is the internationally bestselling author of *The Rosie Project*, *The Rosie Effect*, *The Rosie Result* and *The Best of Adam Sharp*.

May 2019 | Paperback | $16.99 | 9781925773828 | Text Publishing
June 2019 | Hardcover | $26.99 | 9781925773811 | Text Publishing

CONVERSATION STARTERS

1. Much of the humor in the Rosie books comes from Don misreading social situations and cues. How does Simsion make us laugh at Don's interpretations, and the comedy that follows, without making us laugh at Don himself?

2. Don has previously not seen himself as autistic. Why does that change in *The Rosie Result*?

3. How do you think changes in popular understanding of autism, in the years since the first Rosie book was published, are reflected in *The Rosie Result*?

4. When trying to assess whether Hudson is on the autism spectrum, Don considers common ideas about how autistic people behave. How do Don, Hudson, and Blanche conform to, and challenge, stereotypes?

5. Rosie imitates Don as a "sign that she's in a good mood." (2) Does Rosie make fun of Don? Is that okay? Does Rosie seem happy, in her relationship with Don?

6. Reflecting on his parenting, Don thinks about what he would have wanted at Hudson's age: "I would have wanted to be treated as an adult ... to be properly informed, listened to, and involved in decisions affecting me." (73) Is this what most children want? Is it possible to give it to them?

7. Professor Lawrence tells Don that as a "straight, white, middle-aged male who's spent his life in top western universities", he is "the definition of privilege." (23) Do you agree? Does his autism affect his status?

8. One of the book's themes is the sexism encountered by working women. What do you think the novel says about women's roles?

9. Don had previously seen social skills as unimportant, but comes to see a deficit in social skills as potentially damaging. (60) What do you think? What purpose do social skills serve?

10. Don's spent a lifetime trying to fit in, but realizes he doesn't want Hudson to have to do the same. (368) How much should people—autistic or neurotypical—try to "fit in" and modify their behavior to get along with others? Or should the world accommodate difference better?

SAINT X
Alexis Schaitkin

Claire is only seven years old when her college-age sister, Alison, disappears on the last night of their family vacation at a resort on the Caribbean island of Saint X. Several days later, Alison's body is found in a remote spot on a nearby cay, and two local men—employees at the resort—are arrested. Years later, Claire is living and working in New York City when a brief but fateful encounter brings her together with Clive Richardson, one of the men originally suspected of murdering her sister.

As Claire doggedly shadows Clive, hoping to gain his trust, waiting for the slip that will uncover the truth, an unlikely attachment develops between them, two people whose lives were forever marked by the same tragedy.

"Saint X *is slightly miraculous. Funny, chilling, moving, and throughout, deeply intelligent. We follow Emily into the depths of her obsessive quest with fascination and, in the end, rise with her as she moves on. This is an utterly original and engrossing novel written with the surest possible hand."* —**Christopher Tilghman, Author of** *Thomas and Beal in the Midi*

"Here is a marvel of a book, a kaleidoscopic examination of race and privilege, family and self, told with the propulsive, kinetic focus of a crime thriller. Brilliant and unflinching, Saint X *marks the debut of a stunningly gifted writer. I simply couldn't stop reading."* —**Chang-rae Lee, Author of** *On Such A Full Sea*

ABOUT THE AUTHOR: **Alexis Schaitkin**'s short stories and essays have appeared in *Ecotone*, *Southwest Review*, *The Southern Review*, *The New York Times*, and elsewhere. Her fiction has been anthologized in *The Best American Short Stories* and *The Best American Nonrequired Reading*. She received her MFA in fiction from the University of Virginia, where she was a Henry Hoyns Fellow. She lives in Williamstown, Massachusetts, with her husband and son. *Saint X* is her debut novel.

February 2020 | Hardcover | $26.99 | 9781250219596 | Celadon Books

CONVERSATION STARTERS

1. What does the island setting contribute to the story? What about the juxtaposition of New York City?

2. What do you think Claire's habit of writing words in the air with her finger demonstrates about her?

3. What's the symbolism of Faraway Cay and the woman with hooves for feet? What does that mythology add to the story?

4. Why do you think the author chose to intersperse the voices of minor characters, such as the movie actor and other vacationers, throughout the book? What effect does this achieve?

5. What does Claire's name change to Emily signify to you?

6. Did you ever think Clive might pose a threat to Emily when he found out who she was?

7. What does Clive's nickname Gogo indicate about his personality? About Edwin's?

8. Emily's world in New York becomes very small after she encounters Clive. Do you think that was intentional or unintentional on her part? What might have motivated her to turn inward?

9. What do Alison's recorded diary entries reveal to Emily? Was Emily right to listen to them, or do you think it was an invasion of privacy? What about their mom?

10. What are the similarities between Emily's life in New York and Clive's? What are the differences?

11. What do you think about Edwin's relationship with Sara?

12. Alison witnessed a pivotal moment in Clive and Edwin's relationship. How did that shape the rest of the narrative--Clive and Edwin's relationship, their futures, Alison's tragedy?

13. When Emily learns the truth, and remembers the night before Alison disappeared, what do you think is her primary emotion? Grief? Relief? Guilt? Something else?

14. Do you think Emily coming into Clive's life was ultimately a bad thing or a good thing for Clive?

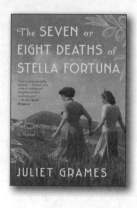

THE SEVEN OR EIGHT DEATHS OF STELLA FORTUNA
Juliet Grames

From Calabria to Connecticut: a sweeping family saga about sisterhood, secrets, Italian immigration, the American dream, and one woman's tenacious fight against her own fate.

For Stella Fortuna, death has always been a part of life. Stella's childhood is full of strange, life-threatening incidents—moments where ordinary situations like cooking eggplant or feeding the pigs inexplicably take lethal turns.

In her rugged Italian village, Stella is considered an oddity—beautiful and smart, insolent and cold. Stella uses her peculiar toughness to protect her slower, plainer baby sister Tina from life's harshest realities. But she also provokes the ire of her father Antonio: a man who demands subservience from women and whose greatest gift to his family is his absence.

When the Fortunas emigrate to America on the cusp of World War II, Stella and Tina must come of age side-by-side in a hostile new world with strict expectations for each of them. Soon Stella learns that her survival is worthless without the one thing her family will deny her at any cost: her independence.

In present-day Connecticut, one family member tells this heartrending story, determined to understand the persisting rift between the now-elderly Stella and Tina.

"Achieves what no sweeping history lesson about American immigrants could: It brings to life a woman that time and history would have ignored." **—Washington Post**

"Epic in scale and richly detailed …. Grames holds the reader under a spell from start to finish." **—O, the Oprah Magazine**

"If you're going through Elena Ferrante withdrawals, this is the book for you." **—Harper's Bazaar**

ABOUT THE AUTHOR: **Juliet Grames** was born in Hartford, Connecticut, and grew up in a tight-knit Italian-American family. A book editor, she has spent the last decade at Soho Press, where she is Associate Publisher and curator of the Soho Crime imprint. This is her first novel.

May 2019 | Hardcover | $27.99 | 9780062862822 | Ecco
April 2020 | Paperback | $17.99 | 9780062862839 | Ecco

CONVERSATION STARTERS

1. Do you think that any of Stella's near-deaths was her own fault? Do you think Stella ever secretly blamed herself for a bad thing that happened to her? Did her family ever blame her?

2. The longer she is married, the more Assunta struggles with her oath to God that she will obey her husband. What individual events reshape her attitude, and how?

3. Do you—or could you—believe in the Evil Eye? Do you think other people's jealousy can take form and negatively affect us?

4. Is Stella a religious person? How does her religiosity differ from her mother's?

5. Does Stella Fortuna's life have a love story? Why do you think there is never a more traditional romance during the course of her long life? Who does Stella love most? Who loves Stella most?

6. If Antonio Fortuna lived today instead of a century ago, would he be considered a sociopath, or is he more complicated? Why do you think he does the abusive things he does?

7. When Stella first experiences her nightmare, she distracts her family from what really happened by blaming an imaginary black man. Why do you think she does this? Do you think Stella's instinct to blame a black man is a product of the time, or do you think she'd do the same today?

8. Stella knows that her father would not want to be identified as one of the "old world" un-Americanized Italians in Hartford. In your opinion, do the Fortunas Americanize, or do they ghettoize themselves among other Italians? Which of the family members do you imagine felt more of a moral imperative to modernize or preserve traditions? Have you observed similar tensions of identity among immigrant groups you may be a part of?

9. Is Carmelo Maglieri a good man?

10. After her Accident, when Stella turns on Tina, what do you think Tina thinks? Do you think she is baffled and heartbroken, or do you think on some level she feels guilty?

SHE WOULD BE KING
Wayétu Moore

A Sarah Jessica Parker Pick for ALA Book Club Central

This powerful debut novel reimagines the dramatic story of Liberia's early years through three unforgettable characters who share an uncommon bond. Gbessa, exiled from the West African village of Lai, is starved, bitten by a viper, and left for dead, but she survives. June Dey, raised on a plantation in Virginia, hides his unusual strength until a confrontation with the overseer forces him to flee. Norman Aragon, the child of a white British colonizer and a Maroon slave from Jamaica, can fade from sight at will, just as his mother could. When the three meet in the settlement of Monrovia, their gifts help them salvage the tense relationship between the African American settlers and the indigenous tribes, as a new nation forms around them.

Moore's intermingling of history and magical realism finds voice not just in these three characters but also in the spirit of the wind, who embodies an ancient wisdom. "If she was not a woman," the wind says of Gbessa, "she would be king." This vibrant story of the African diaspora illuminates the tumultuous roots of a country inextricably bound to the United States.

"Reading Wayétu Moore's debut novel, She Would Be King, *feels a lot like watching a superb athlete's performance ... [Moore] has tapped into her own backstory—and emerged with literary superpowers." —TIME*

"[A] bold début. ... The force and the symbolism of myth pervade Moore's engrossing tale." —The New Yorker

ABOUT THE AUTHOR: **Wayétu Moore** is the founder of One Moore Book and is a graduate of Howard University, Columbia University, and the University of Southern California. Her memoir, *The Dragons, the Giant, the Women*, is forthcoming from Graywolf in June 2020. She teaches at the City University of New York's John Jay College and lives in Brooklyn.

September 2019 | Paperback | $16.00 | 9781644450017 | Graywolf Press

CONVERSATION STARTERS

1. *She Would Be King* is a work of fiction that incorporates historical events. What do the fictional elements add to the portrayal of the founding of Liberia, or of the transatlantic slave trade?

2. The narrating presence of the wind both cautions and comforts the characters in the novel. How does this presence change the way the entire novel is read?

3. With its many narrative threads and points of view, what does *She Would Be King* reveal about the power of storytelling?

4. How does the magical realism employed in *She Would Be King* relate to recent pop culture representations of African and African American superheroes, such as Black Panther and Luke Cage? How do these characters' special abilities align with the reality of the communities to which they belong?

5. Gbessa's relationship to her Vai heritage changes when she joins the settlement in Monrovia. What are the tensions between the cultures? Is Gbessa successful in balancing her various allegiances?

6. Much of the conflict in the book springs from encounters between insiders and outsiders: the way of life in the West African villages is threatened by American settlers and French slavers alike, and Gbessa is branded as an outsider from the moment of her birth. What does *She Would Be King* have to say about suspicion or acceptance of outsiders?

7. Gbessa is set apart from June Dey and Norman Aragon in several ways, and some of those have to do with the fact that Gbessa is a woman. What challenges do the female characters face that the men in the book do not? What strengths do these characters have that set them apart?

8. What role does motherhood play in the novel? How do the various characters experience kinship and lineage?

9. The author's note at the beginning of the novel describes a story that inspired the writing of *She Would Be King*. In what ways does this seed of inspiration take root in the narrative?

10. How would you characterize the ending of *She Would Be King?* Somber or hopeful? Resolved or open-ended?

THE STORYTELLER
Pierre Jarawan

Samir leaves the safety and comfort of his family's adopted home in Germany for volatile Beirut in an attempt to find his missing father. His only clues are an old photo and the bedtime stories his father used to tell him. *The Storyteller* follows Samir's search for Brahim, the father whose heart was always yearning for his homeland, Lebanon. In this moving and gripping novel about family secrets, love, and friendship, Pierre Jarawan does for Lebanon what Khaled Hosseini's *The Kite Runner* did for Afghanistan. He pulls away the curtain of grim facts and figures to reveal the intimate story of an exiled family torn apart by civil war and guilt. In this rich and skilful account, Jarawan proves that he too is a masterful storyteller.

*"A pacy Lebanese mystery... A man is haunted by his father's disappearance in this acclaimed debut novel set against the backdrop of Middle Eastern politics." —**The Guardian***

"As in the iconic 1001 Nights, *storytelling is not just a form of entertainment, but a solution to a problem, a form of appeasement that holds at bay powerful and dangerous forces." —Asymptote*

ABOUT THE AUTHOR: **Pierre Jarawan** was born in 1985 to a Lebanese father and a German mother and moved to Germany with his family at the age of three. Inspired by his father's imaginative bedtime stories, he started writing at the age of thirteen. He has won international prizes as a slam poet, and in 2016 was named Literature Star of the Year by the daily newspaper *Abendzeitung*. Jarawan received a literary scholarship from the City of Munich (the Bayerischer Kunstförderpreis) for *The Storyteller*, which went on to become a bestseller and booksellers' favorite in Germany and the Netherlands.

April 2019 | Paperback | $17.99 | 9781642860115 | World Editions

CONVERSATION STARTERS

1. *The Storyteller* is set in both Germany and Lebanon: how do these two countries compare (and contrast) within the novel?

2. Compare the reactions of Samir and his mother to losing their father/husband. Do they express their grief in similar ways? Does their way of grieving seem healthy? Is it something you have any control over?

3. Samir goes to Lebanon to look for his father. Do you think this was a good idea? Why? Why not?

4. Other than his father, what did he hope to find there?

5. Do you think Samir's father was right to return to Lebanon? Why/why not?

6. Who are the people that helped Samir in his journey? In what ways did they help?

7. What defines the terms "family" and "home"?

8. The history of Lebanon is a central part of the book: What do you know about the current affairs of this region? And, from the events referred to in the book itself, what do you think the main problems are in Lebanon, and can you see any solutions? How does this compare to your country?

9. How do you think Samir feels upon his return to Germany? What do you think the future holds for him?

10. What can you say about Samir's mother's relationship to the other members of her family? Do you think she enjoyed living in Germany? Do you think she also longed to return to Lebanon? Why?

11. In what ways were Yasmin's and Samir's experiences in Germany the same? In what ways do they differ?

12. Following the death of their mother, Samir's sister was taken to a foster family while Samir was left with a friend of the family, Hakim. Was this the best thing for Samir? What else could have been done in this situation?

13. This book also testifies to the power of storytelling, and to an oral storytelling tradition. What does Jarawan have to say about the importance of stories? What are stories able to do for us?

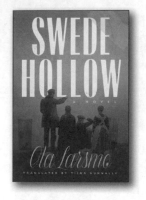

SWEDE HOLLOW
Ola Larsmo and Tiina Nunnally (Translator)

When the Klar family leaves Sweden for New York in 1897, they take with them a terrible secret and a longing for a new life. Their dream of starting over is nearly crushed at the outset, until an unexpected gift allows them to make one more desperate move, this time to the Midwest and a place called Swede Hollow.

Their new home is a cluster of shacks on the edge of St. Paul, Minnesota inhabited by other immigrants. The men hire on as day laborers or work at the nearby brewery, and the women clean houses or work in factories. Outsiders malign Swede Hollow as unsanitary and dangerous, but the Klar family and their neighbors persevere in this neglected corner of the city—and consider it home.

Extensively researched and beautifully written, Ola Larsmo's award-winning novel vividly portrays a family and a community determined to survive. There are hardships and indignities, but also acts of kindness and moments of joy. This haunting story of a real place echoes the larger challenges of immigration in the twentieth century and today.

"A sober and realistic portrayal of the suffering and hardships that awaited Swedish immigrants in America, Swede Hollow *is a moving, at times harrowing, always convincing novel on a truly epic scale."* —**Steve Sem-Sandberg, author of** *The Emperor of Lies*

"A rich and compelling read addressing the basic question of immigration: how does one make a life in a new country?" —**Mary Logue, author of the Claire Watkins mysteries**

"Ola Larsmo writes with sympathy and grace, and his tale is a quiet epic, full of wonder and dreams and loss. Not to be missed." —**Larry Millett, author of** *Metropolitan Dreams*

ABOUT THE AUTHOR: **Ola Larsmo** is a critic and columnist for Sweden's largest newspaper, *Dagens Nyheter*, and the award-winning author of nine novels and several collections of short stories and essays. He has been president of PEN Sweden and editor of *Bonniers Literary Magazine*. **Tiina Nunnally** is an award-winning translator of Norwegian, Danish, and Swedish literature, including Sigrid Undset's novels *Kristin Lavransdatter*, *Jenny*, and *Marta Oulie*.

October 2019 | Hardcover | $26.95 | 9781517904517 | University of Minnesota Press

CONVERSATION STARTERS

1. Why are Gustaf and Anna not seeing eye-to-eye about where they should be going once they reach the States? What might their different reasons be? Why is it so hard to discuss?

2. In New York, why is Gustaf so upset when he realizes that the Norwegian's stool is not in the alley anymore?

3. The Klar family is lucky to see a familiar face at the railway depot in St. Paul when they run into the older Gavin boy, but why do the Swedes have such a hard time communicating with their Irish neighbors in the Hollow? Is it just language issues, or are there more barriers than that?

4. What are the differences between the Swedes down in the Hollow and other Scandinavians living "up on the street?"

5. The "love story" between David and Agnes Karin is in many ways a driving force in the story. But how does it affect the other people around them? What influence does it have on the fate of the Klar family? What about Inga and Jonathan?

6. Did "Ola Värmlänning" really exist? No one in Sweden has ever heard of him, but the stories about him are still being told among descendants of Swedish immigrants in Minnesota and Illinois. Where do these stories come from? What function do they have in an immigrant society? Can you think of any similar stories you might have heard?

7. What role does religion play in the lives of the inhabitants in the Hollow?

8. What part did Carl Hammerberg really play during the lynchings and murders in Duluth? Was it appropriate or unfair that he received a prison sentence? *(The background to the lynchings, and documents from the legal proceedings, can be found on the Minnesota Historical Society's website.)*

9. How do you perceive the "love story" between Ellen and Sol? Is it love? What different needs do they have?

10. Do the relationships between the different ethnic groups in the Hollow change over time? How? What's it like in the Hollow today?

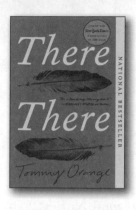

THERE THERE
Tommy Orange

One of the Best Books of the Year: *The Washington Post*, NPR, *Time, O, The Oprah Magazine, The Dallas Morning News, GQ, Entertainment Weekly*, BuzzFeed, *San Francisco Chronicle, The Boston Globe*

Winner of the PEN/Hemingway Award

Winner of the National Book Critics Circle John Leonard Prize

Winner of the Center for Fiction First Novel Prize

Tommy Orange's shattering novel follows twelve characters from Native communities: all traveling to the Big Oakland Powwow, all connected to each other in ways they may not yet realize. Together, this chorus of voices tells of the plight of the urban Native American—grappling with a complex and painful history, with an inheritance of beauty and spirituality, with communion and sacrifice and heroism. Hailed as an instant classic, *There There* is at once poignant and laugh-out-loud funny, utterly contemporary and always unforgettable.

"*Powerful. ...* There There *has so much jangling energy and brings so much news from a distinct corner of American life that it's a revelation.*" —**The New York Times**

"*An astonishing literary debut.*" —**Margaret Atwood**

"*Pure soaring beauty.*" —**The New York Times Book Review**

ABOUT THE AUTHOR: **Tommy Orange** s a graduate of the MFA program at the Institute of American Indian Arts. An enrolled member of the Cheyenne and Arapaho Tribes of Oklahoma, he was born and raised in Oakland, California.

May 2019 | Paperback | $16.00 | 9780525436140 | Vintage

CONVERSATION STARTERS

1. The prologue of *There There* provides a historical overview of how Native populations were systematically stripped of their identity, their rights, their land, and, in some cases, their very existence by colonialist forces in America. How did reading this section make you feel? How does the prologue set the tone for the reader? Discuss the use of the Indian head as iconography. How does this relate to the erasure of Native identity in American culture?

2. Discuss the development of the "Urban Indian" identity and ownership of that label. How does it relate to the push for assimilation by the United States government? How do the characters in *There There* navigate this modern form of identity alongside their ancestral roots?

3. Consider the following statement from page 9: "We stayed because the city sounds like a war, and you can't leave a war once you've been, you can only keep it at bay." In what ways does the historical precedent for violent removal of Native populations filter into the modern era? How does violence—both internal and external—appear throughout the narrative?

4. On page 7, Orange states: "We've been defined by everyone else and continue to be slandered despite easy-to-look-up-on-the-internet facts about the realities of our histories and current state as a people." Discuss this statement in relation to how Native populations have been defined in popular culture. How do the characters in *There There* resist the simplification and flattening of their cultural identity? Relate the idea of preserving cultural identity to Dene Oxendene's storytelling mission.

5. Tony Loneman's perspective both opens and closes *There There*. Why do you think Orange made this choice for the narrative? What does Loneman's perspective reveal about the "Urban Indian" identity? About the landscape of Oakland?

6. When readers are first introduced to Dene Oxendene, we learn of his impulse to tag various spots around the city. How did you interpret this act? How does graffiti culture work to recontextualize public spaces?

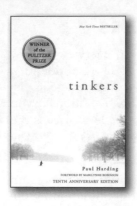

TINKERS
10TH ANNIVERSARY EDITION
Paul Harding
Foreword by Marilynne Robinson

Pulitzer Prize Winner

American Booksellers Association 2019 Indie Next List for Reading Groups selection

American Library Association Notable Book

New York Times **Best Seller**

Special edition of the Pulitzer Prize–winning debut novel–featuring a new foreword by Marilynne Robinson and book club extras inside

In this deluxe tenth anniversary edition, Marilynne Robinson introduces the beautiful novel *Tinkers*, which begins with an old man who lies dying. As time collapses into memory, he travels deep into his past, where he is reunited with his father and relives the wonder and pain of his impoverished New England youth. At once heartbreaking and life affirming, *Tinkers* is an elegiac meditation on love, loss, and the fierce beauty of nature.

"A powerful celebration of life in which a New England father and son, through suffering and joy, transcend their imprisoning lives and offer new ways of perceiving the world and mortality." —**Pulitzer Prize citation**

"Tinkers is truly remarkable. . . . It confers on the reader the best privilege fiction can afford, the illusion of ghostly proximity to other human souls." —**Marilynne Robinson, author of** *Gilead*

"Tinkers is not just a novel—though it is a brilliant novel. It's an instruction manual on how to look at nearly everything. Harding takes the back off to show you the miraculous ticking of the natural world, the world of clocks, generations of family, an epileptic brain, the human soul." —**Elizabeth McCracken, author of** *Bowlaway*

"Keep[s] a reader coming back ... Like Faulkner, [Harding] never shies away from describing what seems impossible to put into words." —**Dallas Morning News**

ABOUT THE AUTHOR: **Paul Harding** is the author of two novels about multiple generations of a New England family: *Enon* and the Pulitzer Prize–winning *Tinkers*.

January 2019 | Paperback | $16.99 | 9781942658603 | Bellevue Literary Press

CONVERSATION STARTERS

1. *Tinkers* is told over the course of eight days, as George lies dying— approximately the same amount of time it takes a hand-wound clock to run down. What do clocks symbolize in *Tinkers*, and why do you think their care and repair is so important to George?

2. George is very tolerant and forgiving of his mother's bitterness toward his father's illness. What do you think accounts for this? What other roles does illness play in the story? How does it draw the characters together or pull them apart?

3. How do the secrets the family keeps from each other affect the way they interact? How do those secrets color their worldview?

4. The spirituality in this novel is subtle but profound. What do you think the author is trying to say about forgiveness, grace, love, and free will?

5. The author, a former drummer, has said that his experience in a band helped him "keep the time" in this novel. Do you sense that rhythm within the story, and is it the kind of novel you'd expect from a rock musician?

6. The narrative is nonlinear, circling back upon the present day as George explores his own memories and as the histories of his father and grandfather are slowly revealed. By telling the story this way and by merely suggesting certain events and leaving other subjects open-ended, do you feel the author succeeds in inviting readers to open their own imaginations and fully participate in and experience the book?

7. The role that kindness plays in the novel is very evocative. How do the passages about the hermit who returned Howard's kindness with his most precious belonging affect your understanding of both characters? What other acts of kindness are performed in the book?

8. In what ways do you see this novel fitting into other classic and contemporary stories of the American experience?

TODAY WE GO HOME
Kelli Estes

Seattle, Washington: Larkin Bennett has always known her place, whether it's surrounded by her loving family in the lush greenery of the Pacific Northwest or conducting a dusty patrol in Afghanistan. But all of that changed the day tragedy struck her unit and took away everything she held dear. Soon after, Larkin discovers an unexpected treasure—the diary of Emily Wilson, a young woman who disguised herself as a man to fight for the Union in the Civil War. As Larkin struggles to heal, she finds herself drawn deeply into Emily's life and the secrets she kept.

Indiana, 1861: The only thing more dangerous to Emily Wilson than a rebel soldier is the risk of her own comrades in the Union Army discovering her secret. But in the minds of her fellow soldiers, if it dresses like a man, swears like a man, and shoots like a man, it must be a man. As the war marches on and takes its terrible toll, Emily begins to question everything she thought she was fighting for.

"Estes passionately brings the past to life, interweaving the story of two women from different centuries whose journey towards hope is timeless." —**Gwendolyn Womack,** *USA Today* **bestselling author of** *The Fortune Teller* **and** *The Time Collector*

"Illuminating, sympathetic, and deeply human… shines a much-needed light on the brave, bold women of all eras." —**Greer Macallister, author of** *The Magicians Lie* **and** *Woman 99*

ABOUT THE AUTHOR: **Kelli Estes** is the author of *The Girl Who Wrote in Silk.* She lived in the deserts of Washington state and Arizona before settling in the Seattle area. She's passionate about stories that help us see how the past shapes who we are today, and how we all have more in common than not.

September 2019 | Paperback | $15.99 | 9781492664185 | Sourcebooks Landmark

CONVERSATION STARTERS

1. A major theme of the story explores the female soldier's experience. Did any of these women's experiences surprise you? If you have any military experience, what are some major challenges, prejudices, abuses, etc. that you experienced as a female military member or witnessed by other women in the military?

2. Opening all military jobs to women in recent years has started the debate on whether women should be included in any future drafts/conscriptions. What do you think?

3. The epigraph at the beginning of the book reads "Home isn't where our house is, but wherever we are understood." Emily's home was in Indiana, yet it stopped being a place where people truly knew her. Larkin grew up in Seattle but chose to go home to Woodinville because that's where she felt best loved. What does home mean to you? Where is your "home" and why do you call it home?

4. There are people today who still don't believe the Civil War was about slavery. What do you think, and why?

5. Was it a surprise to you to learn that black men were not allowed to join the Union army until 1863? That they were segregated from white soldiers and led exclusively by white officers? That they were not paid the same wages as white soldiers until June 1864? That, if caught by Confederate forces, they were usually brutally killed and never taken prisoner? Do you think the war might have ended sooner if any of these facts were different?

6. Through most of the story, Emily's family is made up of her brother and Willie. For Larkin, it is her grandmother and cousins. Both women have other family members, but they feel emotionally disconnected from them. Who do you consider your true family, no matter if they are actual family? What is it about these people that you love so much?

7. Emily's diary directly influenced Sarah's decision to join the military. Imagine one of your ancestors left a diary detailing his or her experiences during an interesting time in history. What would you do with that information? Share with the group what you already know about your ancestor and how he/she lived. How might learning more about this ancestor's experiences through a diary affect you?

TRUST EXERCISE
Susan Choi

In the early 1980s, students at a highly competitive performing arts high school struggle and thrive in a rarified bubble, ambitiously pursuing their acting. When two freshmen, David and Sarah, fall headlong into love, their passion does not go unnoticed—or untoyed with—by anyone, especially not by their charismatic teacher, Mr. Kingsley.

The outside world fails to penetrate this school's walls—until it does, in a shocking spiral of events that catapults the action forward in time and flips the premise upside-down. What the reader believes to have happened to David and Sarah and their friends is not entirely true—though it's not false, either. It takes until the book's stunning coda for the final piece of the puzzle to fall into place—revealing truths that will resonate long after the final sentence.

As captivating and tender as it is surprising, Susan Choi's *Trust Exercise* will incite heated conversations about fiction and truth, and about friendships and loyalties, and will leave readers with wiser understandings of the true capacities of adolescents and of the powers and responsibilities of adults.

"Book groups, meet your next selection. ... Trust Exercise *is fiction that contains multiple truths and lies ... Choi has produced something uncommonly thought-provoking."* —**NPR**

"This psychologically acute novel enlists your heart as well as your mind. [A] delicious and, in its way, rather delicate ... phosphorescent examination of sexual consent." —**The New York Times**

ABOUT THE AUTHOR: **Susan Choi** is author of the novels *My Education*, *A Person of Interest*, *American Woman*, and *The Foreign Student*. Her work has been a finalist for the Pulitzer Prize and the PEN/Faulkner Award and winner of the PEN/W.G. Sebald Award and the Asian-American Literary Award for fiction. With David Remnick, she co-edited *Wonderful Town: New York Stories* from *The New Yorker*. She's received NEA and Guggenheim Foundation fellowships. She lives in Brooklyn.

April 2019 | Hardcover | $27.00 | 9781250309884 | Henry Holt & Company

CONVERSATION STARTERS

1. Driving is a central theme throughout the first section of the book. What would a car and more freedom mean for Sarah and David? Does the ability to drive signify something beyond the ability to drive away from uncomfortable situations, and how would the story change if the characters could drive?

2. Ms. Rozot is new to the school and comforts Sarah after she breaks down. She tells Sarah that young people experience emotional pain more intensely than adults do. Has this been true in your own experience?

3. Sarah chooses to write about her high school experiences, though her version seems to differ from the actual events. What are some clues early on that Sarah's story is not completely true?

4. The story breaks suddenly in the middle of the book. Were you able to stay grounded in the new sections?

5. Sarah makes the choice to make Mr. Kingsley gay in her version of the story, but in reality he is straight. How does this change the interactions he has with his female students?

6. How reliable of a narrator do we find Karen, versus Sarah? Do you think that either of their stories is accurate?

7. Though the novel is set far before the #MeToo movement, its exploration of consent and what it means to be a young person influenced by people in power is relevant to our conversations about consent today. How does this book illuminate those conversations, and what does it mean for a teenager to consent to adult situations in any era?

8. The characters in *Trust Exercise* often seem much older than fifteen in terms of sexuality and romantic relationships. Do you think older Sarah is embellishing her past sexuality to shock readers of her novel, or do we discount teenage sexuality as we get older?

9. How does *Trust Exercise* differ in its portrayal of a performing arts high school from previous portrayals, such as those in *Fame* or *Glee*?

10. Could the book be arranged differently? How might that change the way we read the story, and the extent to which we trust each narrator?

WASHINGTON BLACK
Esi Edugyan

One of the Best Books of the Year: *The Boston Globe*, *The Washington Post*, *Time*, *Entertainment Weekly*, *San Francisco Chronicle*, *Financial Times*, *Minneapolis Star Tribune*, NPR, *The Economist*, *Bustle*, *The Dallas Morning News*, *Slate*, *Kirkus Reviews*

One of Barack Obama's Favorite Books of the Year

Eleven-year-old George Washington Black—or Wash—a field slave on a Barbados sugar plantation, is initially terrified when he is chosen as the manservant of his master's brother. To his surprise, however, the eccentric Christopher Wilde turns out to be a naturalist, explorer, inventor, and abolitionist. Soon Wash is initiated into a world where a flying machine can carry a man across the sky, where even a boy born in chains may embrace a life of dignity and meaning, and where two people, separated by an impossible divide, can begin to see each other as human.

But when a man is killed and a bounty is placed on Wash's head, they must abandon everything and flee together. Over the course of their travels, what brings Wash and Christopher together will tear them apart, propelling Wash ever farther across the globe in search of his true self. Spanning the Caribbean to the frozen Far North, London to Morocco, *Washington Black* is a story of self-invention and betrayal, of love and redemption, and of a world destroyed and made whole again.

"A daring work of empathy and imagination." —*The New York Times Book Review*

"A gripping historical narrative exploring both the bounds of slavery and what it means to be truly free." —*Vanity Fair*

ABOUT THE AUTHOR: **Esi Edugyan** is author of the novels *The Second Life of Samuel Tyne* and *Half-Blood Blues*, which won the Scotiabank Giller Prize and was a finalist for the Man Booker Prize, the Governor General's Literary Award, the Rogers Writers' Trust Fiction Prize and the Orange Prize. She lives in Victoria, British Columbia.

April 2019 | Paperback | $16.95 | 9780525563242 | Vintage

CONVERSATION STARTERS

1. Big Kit tells Washington that "If you dead, you wake up again in your homeland. You wake up free." How does this line resonate at the end of the book, in the final moments as Wash asks about Dahomey and looks out into the horizon?

2. Why do you think Big Kit didn't tell Wash that she was his mother? Do you think he would have responded to Titch's offer differently had he known? How might his life have been different?

3. Wash describes his scar from the explosion with the Cloud Cutter as "the utter destruction [that] his act had now wrought upon my life." Discuss the kinds of scars the characters sustain in the novel, both visible and invisible.

4. Tanna tells Wash, "You are like an interruption in a novel, Wash. The agent that sets things off course. Like a hailstorm. Or a wedding." How does this metaphor manifest in literal and symbolic ways throughout Wash's journeys?

5. What does it mean to be a "master" in this time period and for these characters? Recall Wash's first impression of Philip as "the oddity of a body used for nothing but satisfying urges, bloated and ethereal as sea foam, as if it might break apart. He smelled of molasses and salted cod, and of the fine sweetness of mangoes in the hot season."

6. Part of what Titch first notices in Wash is an uncanny gift for drawing. How does the ability to observe and record run through the novel as a motif? What becomes, as Titch says, "worthy of observation"?

7. What draws Wash to the beauty of the octopus? What does it mean for him, a former slave, to capture it and other specimens for study and display, even with the motive of showing people that creatures they thought were "nightmarish . . . were in fact beautiful and nothing to fear"?

8. The novel is set between 1830 and 1836 and takes place on multiple continents. How are the larger global and political tremors shaking the world during this time felt through the characters? For example, Titch is described as an Abolitionist and often derided for it. How does this aspect of his worldview affect the way he behaves? What about your perceptions of him as a character?

WE SOLD OUR SOULS
Grady Hendrix

An NPR Pop Culture Happy Hour Pick

An io9 2018 Fall Preview Pick

A 2018 Goodreads Choice Award Finalist

Now in paperback, in this hard-rocking, spine-tingling supernatural thriller, the washed-up guitarist of a '90s heavy metal band embarks on an epic road-trip across America and deep into the web of a sinister conspiracy.

Every morning, Kris Pulaski wakes up in hell. In the 1990s she was lead guitarist of Dürt Würk, a heavy-metal band on the brink of breakout success until lead singer Terry Hunt embarked on a solo career and rocketed to stardom, leaving his bandmates to rot in obscurity.

Now Kris works as night manager of a Best Western; she's tired, broke, and unhappy. One day everything changes—a shocking act of violence turns her life upside down, and she begins to suspect that Terry sabotaged more than just the band. Kris hits the road, hoping to reunite Dürt Würk and confront the man who ruined her life. Her journey will take her from the Pennsylvania rust belt to a celebrity rehab center to a satanic music festival. A furious power ballad about never giving up, *We Sold Our Souls* is one woman's epic journey to reclaim her life—and save her soul.

"A good, creepy, music-tinged thriller." —**CNET**

"The quintessential horror-metal novel for our times." —*Los Angeles Review of Books*

ABOUT THE AUTHOR: Grady Hendrix is a novelist and screenwriter based in New York City. His novels include *Horrorstör*, named one of the best books of 2014 by National Public Radio, and *My Best Friend's Exorcism*, for which the *Wall Street Journal* dubbed him "a national treasure." The Bram Stoker Award winning *Paperbacks from Hell*, a survey of outrageous horror novels of the 1970s and '80s, was called "pure, demented delight" by the *New York Times Book Review*. He's contributed to *Playboy*, *The Village Voice*, and *Variety*.

June 2019 | Paperback | $14.99 | 9781683691242 | Quirk Books

CONVERSATION STARTERS

1. Before reading this book, how much did you know about the music industry generally and heavy metal in particular? Did you learn anything new about either of these subjects?

2. How do the author's depictions of Kris Pulaski playing her guitar function as a storytelling device?

3. How did the culture of heavy metal influence the way that characters deal with or react to the situations in which they find themselves?

4. In what ways are Kris and Melanie Gutiérrez similar? In what ways are they different? Why do you think Melanie chose to help Kris?

5. The two characters whose opinions most strongly clash with those of Terry Hunt are women. Why do you think the author chose to put female characters in opposition to Terry?

6. Why did Melanie want to move to Los Angeles? Can you relate to any of her reasons?

7. The chapters are interrupted by excerpts of radio interviews and commercials and news articles. What purpose did these selections serve? Do you think they enhanced the story?

8. Lyrics from Dürt Würk's songs appear throughout the book. Did the inclusion of song lyrics change your perspective on the narrative? Did you feel like you could "hear" Dürt Würk's music as you read?

9. We learn that Kris experienced traumatic events in the time prior to the start of the novel. What effect do you think these experiences had on her and on her decision making?

10. How did you feel about the author's choice to associate mundane things like UPS delivery drivers and contractual disputes with the sinister forces behind Terry's success?

WELCOME TO AMERICA
Linda Boström Knausgård

Ellen has stopped talking. She thinks she may have killed her dad. Her brother's barricaded himself in his room. Their mother, a successful actress, carries on as normal. "We're a family of light!" she insists. But darkness seeps in everywhere and in their separate worlds each of them longs for togetherness. *Welcome to America* is a dark portrait of a sensitive, strong-willed child in the throes of trauma, and a family on the brink of disaster.

"Knausgård's story of a family in crisis is shocking and imaginative. Everything is written in beautiful and sparse prose which suggests that, after all, from darkness comes light." —**Jury, August Prize**

"Welcome to America presents itself as an étude in the musical sense of the term: a basic theme that varies to infinity, acquiring with each new variation a new unprecedented facet. A triumph." —*Le Monde*

"A tender novel about a mute girl: gentle, sensitive, minimal, concise, subtle, and brutal. This is writing as self-defense and liberation." —**Spiegel**

"A daring and disturbing novel. One will not soon forget the eleven-year-old narrator and her silence." —**MDR Kultur**

"In her slim book, Boström Knausgård conjures a constellation reminiscent of a psychological thriller. Welcome to America is a book that masterfully describes the many nuances of inner darkness." —**Austria Presse Agentur**

"Linda Boström Knausgård erases herself from her own writing. What remains is the girl who communicates directly with the reader in a remarkably strong voice, despite her being so quiet." —**Svenska Dagbladet**

ABOUT THE AUTHOR: **Linda Boström Knausgård** (Sweden) is an author and poet, as well as a producer of documentaries for Swedish radio. Her first novel, *The Helios Disaster*, was awarded the Mare Kandre Prize and shortlisted for the Swedish Radio Novel Award 2014. *Welcome to America*, her second novel, has been awarded the prestigious Swedish August Prize and nominated for the Svenska Dagbladet Literary Prize.

September 2019 | Paperback | $15.99 | 978164286-0412 | World Editions

CONVERSATION STARTERS

1. The author Linda Bostrom Knausgaard says about her recurring theme of silence: "It provokes a lot of reactions. It turns into a space that others want to fill perhaps by speaking even more. It's hard to cope with silence." Discuss the theme of silence, and the ways in which silence can be used as a weapon.

2. Why does Ellen decide to stop speaking, and what do you think she hopes to achieve?

3. Can you describe the relationship between Ellen and her mother?

4. Ellen's brother features somewhat less in the story. Can you describe a little how you imagine his experience of coping with his grief to be?

5. Do you think Ellen's mother and the school are dealing with Ellen in the right way? Why, why not?

6. What would help Ellen?

7. When, if at all, is Ellen happy?

8. What do you imagine for Ellen in the future; will she speak again?

9. Are there moments in the novel where you can see that Ellen wants to speak? What happens in these moments?

10. Did Ellen have a good relationship with her father? Does she miss him?

11. What is the significance of the book's title?

12. Bostrom writes in a very poetic and hypnotic style; how do you think this adds to the experience of the novel?

13. Have you read any similar books before (for example, first-person monologues)? If so, how do they compare? If not, would you consider it now?

WHERE THE DEAD SIT TALKING
Brandon Hobson

Finalist for the 2018 National Book Award for Fiction

NPR's *Code Switch* Best Books of 2018

A *Southern Living* Best Book of 2018

A *Kirkus Reviews* Best Book of 2018

2019 In the Margins Book Award Top Fiction Novel

With his single mother in jail, Sequoyah, a fifteen-year-old Cherokee boy, is placed in foster care with the Troutt family. Literally and figuratively scarred by his mother's years of substance abuse, Sequoyah keeps mostly to himself, living with his emotions pressed deep below the surface. At least until he meets seventeen-year-old Rosemary, a troubled artist who also lives with the family.

Sequoyah and Rosemary bond over their shared Native American background and tumultuous paths through the foster care system, but as Sequoyah's feelings toward Rosemary deepen, the precariousness of their lives and the scars of their pasts threaten to undo them both.

"An extraordinary book." —NPR's *Code Switch*

"A strange and powerful Native American Bildungsroman ... this novel breathes with a dark, pulsing life of its own." —*The Tulsa Voice*

"Soulful." —*Dallas Morning News*

"A sensitive and searching exploration of a youth forged in turbulence ... A thrilling confirmation of Brandon Hobson's immense gifts on the page." —Laura van den Berg, author of *Find Me*

"Authentic and humane." —*The Oklahoman*

"A masterly tale of life and death, hopes and fears, secrets and lies." —*Kirkus Reviews,* starred review

ABOUT THE AUTHOR: **Brandon Hobson** is a recipient of a Pushcart Prize. He is the author of *Desolation of Avenues Untold*, *Deep Ellum*, and *The Levitationist*. He is an enrolled member of the Cherokee Nation Tribe of Oklahoma.

June 2019 | Paperback | $16.00 | 9781641290173 | Soho Press

CONVERSATION STARTERS

1. Sequoyah is a man looking back on a short period in his life when he was a youth in foster care. How is his voice different than a fifteen-year-old telling the story? What details does he add or leave out that a teenager might tell differently?

2. How does Sequoyah's difficult home life affect his relationships with the people he meets?

3. Sequoyah says he would like to be Rosemary and even finds himself sneaking into her room and into her closet to explore. What feelings do you think he is experiencing regarding his own gender or identity?

4. Is Sequoyah a reliable narrator? Why or why not?

5. Does Sequoyah seem dangerous? Why is George afraid of him?

6. How are George and Sequoyah alike as fostered youth? How are they different?

7. In what ways are the Troutts effective (or not effective) foster parents?

8. What role does Sequoyah play in what ultimately happens to Rosemary?

9. How does Sequoyah change from the beginning of the book to the end?

10. How does displacement serve as a central theme to the book? Do foster children like Sequoyah mirror the way Cherokees and other tribes were forced out of their land in the late 1800s before walking the Trail of Tears?

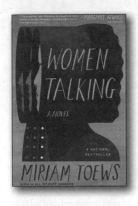

WOMEN TALKING
Miriam Toews

One evening, eight Mennonite women climb into a hay loft to conduct a secret meeting. For the past two years, each of these women, and more than a hundred other women, has been repeatedly violated in the night by demons coming to punish them for their sins. Now that the women have learned they were in fact drugged and attacked by a group of men from their own community, they are determined to protect themselves and their daughters from future harm.

While the men of the colony are off in the city, attempting to raise enough money to bail out the rapists and bring them home, these women—all illiterate, without any knowledge of the world outside their community and unable even to speak the language of the country they live in-have very little time to make a choice: Should they stay in the only world they've ever known or should they dare to escape?

Based on real events and told through the "minutes" of the women's all-female symposium, Toews's masterful novel is a tale of women claiming their own power to decide.

"This amazing, sad, shocking, but touching novel, based on a real-life event, could be right out of The Handmaid's Tale.*"* —**Margaret Atwood, on Twitter**

"Scorching." —New York Times Book Review, **Editor's Choice**

"Astonishing ... Essential, elemental." —USA Today

*"Lean, bristling ... A remarkably layered and gripping story." —**Wall Street Journal***

"The intelligence on display in Women Talking *is as ferocious as it is warm."* —**NPR.org**

ABOUT THE AUTHOR: **Miriam Toews** is the author of six previous bestselling novels, including *All My Puny Sorrows*, and one work of nonfiction, *Swing Low: A Life*. She is winner of the Governor General's Award for Fiction, the Libris Award for Fiction Book of the Year, the Rogers Writers' Trust Fiction Prize, and the Writers' Trust Engel/Findley Award. She lives in Toronto.

April 2019 | Hardcover | $24.00 | 9781635572582 | Bloomsbury

CONVERSATION STARTERS

1. *Women Talking* begins with "A Note on the Novel" which explains that the story is a fictionalized account of real events. What is the difference between reading this novel versus reading a news story or nonfiction book about these events? What questions does Women Talking encourage readers to ask themselves about these events and the environment in which they occur?

2. The book is told through August Epp's notes from the women's meetings. Why does Toews choose Epp to narrate this story? How does his perspective, gender, and personal history affect the vantage from which the story is told?

3. The women frequently discuss the complexity of continuing to love many of the men in their community despite their fear and they contemplate the circumstances under which the men would be allowed to join them in their new society. In what ways does the novel explore questions about male experiences, perspectives, and culture?

4. Which of the options would you have taken if you were one of the women? Explain why. Consider the consequences and benefits of your choice. How would you convince the others to join you?

5. The book examines both sexual and domestic violence. How does the women's environment and circumstances dictate how they understand, interpret, and, ultimately, deal with violence? How does this intersect with their religious faith and their beliefs about their place in the world?

6. Discuss the power of language and literacy. How would the women's lives be changed if they could read? How does their ability to interpret the Bible for themselves change the women's understanding of their future?

7. How does this novel engage with mainstream political and social conversations about women and their rights?

NONFICTION

THE BLINK OF AN EYE: A MEMOIR OF DYING—AND LEARNING HOW TO LIVE AGAIN

Rikke Schmidt Kjærgaard
Foreword by Bill Bryson

A Summer 2019 B&N Discover Great New Writers selection

It was New Year's Day. Rikke Schmidt Kjærgaard, a young mother and scientist, was celebrating with family and friends when she was struck down with a sudden fever. Within hours, she'd suffered multiple organ failure and was clinically dead.

Then, brought back to the edge of life—trapped in a near-death coma from an acute case of bacterial meningitis—she was given a 5 percent chance of survival. She awoke to find herself completely paralyzed, with blinking as her sole means of communication.

The Blink of an Eye is Rikke's gripping account of being locked inside her own body, and what it took to painstakingly relearn every basic life skill—from breathing and swallowing, speaking and walking, to truly *living* again. Much more than an account of recovery against all odds—this is, at its heart, a celebration of love, family, and every little thing that matters when life hangs in the balance.

"A highly personal, deeply affecting account of what it is to be yanked from a happy, well-ordered life and thrust into a sudden, unimaginable, terrifying darkness. Rikke Schmidt Kjærgaard has done the impossible of putting into words an experience that would seem to be beyond expressing."
—from the foreword by Bill Bryson

"A true stunner, unbearably sad yet full of hope." —*Booklist* **(Starred Review)**

"A rich reading experience ... an inspirational story of beating the odds."
—*Kirkus Reviews*

ABOUT THE AUTHOR: **Rikke Schmidt Kjærgaard** is a scientist, mother of three, and cofounder of Graphicure, a start-up developing software that empowers patients to better understand their disease and manage treatment. She is also cofounder and CEO of the Danish Science Club, a mentorship network for children and teens. She holds a PhD in science communication, with past positions as a postdoctoral fellow at MRC Mitochondrial Biology Unit in Cambridge, UK, and at Harvard Medical School.

May 2019 | Paperback | $15.95 | 9781615195718 | The Experiment

CONVERSATION STARTERS

1. In his foreword, Bill Bryson writes, "Rikke has done the impossible of putting into words an experience that would seem to be beyond expressing," and many of the critical reviews echo that amazement of her calm, even humorous, yet terrifyingly detailed account of her illness. (xi) Have you ever experienced that sense of composure during traumatic events, or known people who did?

2. Rikke is able to recall events from when she was dead and in a coma because of Peter's detailed journals. "Writing kept him sane," she states, but it also was key to her recovery, physiologically and psycho-emotionally. (13) Discuss how this remove from her own experiences affects her outlook while in the hospital and rehab, as well as the tone of her writing.

3. Rikke's children are deeply impacted by their mother's ordeal, especially eight-year-old Daniel. How does he inspire Rikke to be "fearless" in her recovery and life post-hospital? (144)

4. There are many moments when Rikke's progress seems to be derailed—by the amputation of her fingers, the infection in her sinuses, the watery eye that the doctor misdiagnoses as depression, etc. What motivated her to not lose faith in these moments, but rather to push through and get well?

5. *Foreword Reviews* claims that "this sharp and unselfpitying account has important information for medical professionals and loved ones about how to care for and support postcoma patients." How is the doctors' care for Rikke described? Have you ever experienced insensitivity from doctors, and what was your response? And on the other hand, have you ever received extraordinary care from a doctor, and, if so, to what do you attribute that extraordinary care?

6. In her *Wall Street Journal* essay, Rikke writes: "I owe my recovery to the non-medical professional who was my proxy: my husband ... Every patient deserves and needs that kind of voice." How has she used this book, the "Caregiver's Checklist" at the end, and her company, Graphicure, to provide a voice for patients like herself? Have you ever been in a situation where you needed someone else to speak for you?

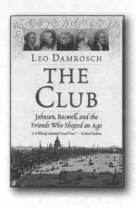

THE CLUB: JOHNSON, BOSWELL, AND THE FRIENDS WHO SHAPED AN AGE

Leo Damrosch

Prize-winning biographer Leo Damrosch tells the story of "the Club," a group of extraordinary writers, artists, and thinkers who gathered weekly at a London tavern

In 1763, the painter Joshua Reynolds proposed to his friend Samuel Johnson that they invite a few friends to join them every Friday at the Turk's Head Tavern in London to dine, drink, and talk until midnight. Eventually the group came to include among its members Edmund Burke, Adam Smith, Edward Gibbon, and James Boswell. It was known simply as "the Club."

In this captivating book, Leo Damrosch brings alive a brilliant, competitive, and eccentric cast of characters. With the friendship of the "odd couple" Samuel Johnson and James Boswell at the heart of his narrative, Damrosch conjures up the precarious, exciting, and often brutal world of late eighteenth-century Britain. This is the story of an extraordinary group of people whose ideas helped to shape their age, and our own.

"A magnificently entertaining book." —**Michael Dirda,** *Washington Post*

"Damrosch's magnificent history revives the Club's creative ferment." —***New York Times Book Review,*** **Editors' Choice**

"Impeccable scholarship at the service of absolute lucidity ... Learned, penetrating, a pleasure to read." —**Joseph Epstein,** *Wall Street Journal*

"Engaging and illuminating ... we are transported back to a world of conversations, arguments, ideas, and writings. And in this vibrantly realized milieu, words rarely fail." —**Jenny Uglow,** *New York Review of Books*

ABOUT THE AUTHOR: **Leo Damrosch** is the Ernest Bernbaum Professor of Literature Emeritus at Harvard University. His previous works include the NBCC Award winner *Jonathan Swift: His Life and His World,* and *Eternity's Sunrise: The Imaginative World of William Blake.*

March 2019 | Hardcover | $30.00 | 9780300217902 | Yale University Press

CONVERSATION STARTERS

1. Members of the Club differed in many of their opinions (toward politics, travel, foreigners, the poor, women, etc.), and yet they enjoyed lively discussions and for the most part remained friends. What can we learn from them about maintaining civility?

2. What aspects of eighteenth century life appeal to you? Which customs, attitudes, or laws would seem intolerable?

3. Regardless of talent or education, women were specifically excluded from membership in the Club. Even so, Johnson valued women and had close relationships with several. Can you identify any advantages that women of the times enjoyed? How did they exert influence?

4. What sense do you get of different styles of marriage: loving (Garrick, Boswell), unhappy (Johnson), and polite but unromantic (the Thrales)? How did Boswell rationalize his compulsive recourse to prostitutes?

5. Reynolds promoted the idea of the Club with the intent of relieving Johnson's bouts with depression through lively discussion, food, and drink that fueled weekly Friday night gatherings. Does your reading club or other group resemble the Turk's Head Tavern gatherings in any way?

6. Both Johnson and Boswell suffered difficult childhoods and illnesses while receiving minimal sympathy from their parents. Compare their experiences with those of children today.

7. Do you find the evidence convincing to suggest that Johnson would be diagnosed today with obsessive compulsive disorder, and Boswell with bipolar disorder and alcoholism?

8. If Boswell were contemplating a biography of a public figure or celebrity in the twenty-first century, who would you propose as an interesting subject?

9. Surprisingly, Boswell included Johnson's eloquent argument against slavery in *The Life of Samuel Johnson*, then proceeded to defend the institution using terms like "humane" and "mercy." Does this change your opinion of Boswell? What opinions or positions of our times would you regard as rationalizations?

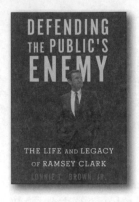

DEFENDING THE PUBLIC'S ENEMY: THE LIFE AND LEGACY OF RAMSEY CLARK

Lonnie T. Brown, Jr.

Defending the Public's Enemy is the first book to explore the enigmatic and perplexing life and legal career of U.S. Attorney General Ramsey Clark. Clark's life and work were enmeshed with some of the most notable people and events of the 1960s: Martin Luther King, Jr., the Watts Riots, the Voting Rights Act, the Black Panthers, and Muhammad Ali. Clark worked tirelessly, especially to secure the civil rights of black Americans. Upon entering the private sector, the former insider became one of his government's staunchest critics, providing legal defense to internationally-despised figures, alleged terrorists, reputed Nazi war criminals, and brutal dictators.

The provocative life chronicled in *Defending the Public's Enemy* personifies the contradictions at the heart of American political history, and our ambivalent relationship with dissenters and marginalized groups, as well as those who embody a fiercely independent revolutionary spirit.

"In this captivating biography, Lonnie T. Brown offers an intimate window into Ramsey Clark's controversial career as it intersected and shaped twentieth-century political and legal history, and challenges how we understand the role of lawyers in a democratic society." —**Anthony Romero, Executive Director, ACLU**

"Both a fascinating account of the man and lawyer and a captivating lens through which to see a connection among important events in contemporary history." —**Bruce Green, Fordham University School of Law**

ABOUT THE AUTHOR: **Lonnie T. Brown, Jr.** is the A. Gus Cleveland Distinguished Chair of Legal Ethics and Professionalism at the University of Georgia School of Law. He specializes in legal ethics and civil procedure, and speaks and publishes widely in the area of legal ethics in the adversary process.

July 2019 | Hardcover | $35.00 | 9781503601390 | Stanford University Press

CONVERSATION STARTERS

1. The book's introduction begins with an epigraph from Ramsey Clark: "Life is full of turbulence and conflict, and I never try to avoid either. In fact, I guess I seek them out because that's where the chance to make a difference is." What kind of picture does this paint of Ramsey Clark's character before you read the book? After reading the book, does this quote help make sense of Clark's actions?

2. A common critique of Ramsey Clark is that he is anti-American; however, he considers himself a patriot, not a traitor. He has said, "If you really love your country, you work hard to make it right ... Anything else is an extreme lack of disloyalty and an extreme failure of courage." Do you agree or disagree with this sentiment?

3. How did President Kennedy's assassination affect Ramsey emotionally? How did it impact the trajectory of his political career?

4. Following the Watts riots, the president gave Ramsey an assignment intended to help "restore and rehabilitate the damaged areas of Los Angeles." What did Ramsey discover after meeting with Watts citizens?

5. Ramsey believes that fear in the general public played a major role in preventing progress in addressing the underlying ills within society, in particular, poverty in the black community. What role do you think fear plays in today's society?

6. Many of Ramsey's actions went against popular opinion and were damaging to his reputation. Have you ever been in a situation in which you stood up for what you believe in, even though the majority of others disagreed with you?

7. The author has pointed out one similarity amongst the people Ramsey has chosen to defend throughout his post-DOJ career. What is the common thread between all these people?

8. Each chapter opens with a quote from Ramsey Clark. Which one do you find the most intriguing, and why?

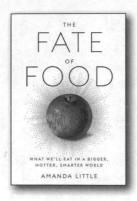

THE FATE OF FOOD: WHAT WE'LL EAT IN A BIGGER, HOTTER, SMARTER WORLD
Amanda Little

In this fascinating look at the race to secure the global food supply, environmental journalist and professor Amanda Little tells the defining story of the sustainable food revolution as she weaves together stories from the world's most creative and controversial innovators on the front lines of food science, agriculture, and climate change.

Climate models show that global crop production will decline every decade for the rest of this century due to drought, heat, and flooding. Water supplies are in jeopardy. Meanwhile, the world's population is expected to grow another 30 percent by midcentury. So how, really, will we feed nine billion people sustainably in the coming decades?

Amanda Little, a professor at Vanderbilt University and an award-winning journalist, spent three years traveling through a dozen countries and as many U.S. states in search of answers to this question.

The race to reinvent the global food system is on, and the challenge is twofold: We must solve the existing problems of industrial agriculture while also preparing for the pressures ahead.

"How will we feed humanity in the era of climate change? Amanda Little tackles an immense topic with grit and optimism in this fast, fascinating read. A beautifully written triumph." —**Former Secretary of State John Kerry**

ABOUT THE AUTHOR: **Amanda Little** is a professor of journalism and Writer-in-Residence at Vanderbilt University. Her reporting on energy, technology, and the environment has taken her to ultra-deep oil rigs, down manholes, and inside monsoon clouds. Little's work has appeared in publications ranging from *The New York Times* and *The Washington Post* to *Wired*, *Rolling Stone*, and *Bloomberg Businessweek*.

June 2019 | Hardcover | $27.00 | 9780804189033 | Harmony

CONVERSATION STARTERS

1. *The Fate of Food*'s take-home message is that the answer to the impending food scarcity crisis might be in a new approach that draws on the wisdom of traditional agriculture and the exciting, emerging technologies of the present. Amanda Little explores startling innovations around the world: farmscrapers, cloned cattle, meatless animal meat, edible insects, super-bananas, and weeding robots. Which of these seem most promising to you, and what are some other ways food and agriculture can adapt to climate change and become more resilient, productive, and sustainable?

2. What did you already know about this book's subject before you read this book? How did it change your understanding of, or expectations for, sustainable and equitable food production going forward? What new things did you learn?

3. Do you think that GMOs crops designed for drought resilience and heat tolerance are a reasonable way to counteract the increasing pressures of climate change on global food production? What are some alternatives?

4. How can we change public opinion on GMOs, especially since a lot of the opposition seems driven by a vision of nature as being pure and vulnerable?

5. In Chapter 4, the robotics expert Jorge Heraud is quoted as saying that "robots don't have to remove us from nature—they can help us restore it." Do you agree? Why or why not?

6. Do you believe the actions Little discusses will be enough to forestall the direct impacts of climate change? Or do you think it's too little too late?

7. Discuss specific passages that struck you as significant, illuminating, disturbing, etc. What was especially memorable for you?

8. How does this book compare to other books or articles on sustainable food systems or climate change that you've read?

9. What topics does the book make you want to explore further?

10. What do you think and hope will be on your family's Thanksgiving table in the year 2050?

FEAST OF ASHES: THE LIFE AND ART OF DAVID OHANNESSIAN

Sato Moughalian

Along the cobbled streets and golden walls of Jerusalem, brilliantly glazed tiles catch the light and beckon the eye. These colorful wares—known as Armenian ceramics—are iconic features of the Holy City. Silently, these works of ceramic art represent a riveting story of resilience and survival.

Feast of Ashes tells the story of David Ohannessian, the renowned ceramicist who in 1919 founded the art of Armenian pottery in Jerusalem, where his work and that of his followers is now celebrated as a local treasure. Ohannessian's life encompassed some of the most tumultuous upheavals of the modern Middle East. Born in an isolated Anatolian mountain village, he witnessed the rise of violent nationalism in the waning years of the Ottoman Empire, endured arrest and deportation in the Armenian Genocide, founded a new ceramics tradition in Jerusalem under the British Mandate, and spent his final years, uprooted, in Cairo and Beirut.

Ohannessian's life story is revealed by his granddaughter Sato Moughalian, weaving together family narratives with newly unearthed archival findings. Witnessing her personal quest for the man she never met, we come to understand a universal story of migration, survival, and hope.

"Feast of Ashes *is a passionate journey of discovery, an exemplary work of craft and design history, and a powerful narrative of the meaning of family identity. An extraordinary book—I loved it.*" —**Edmund de Waal, author of** *The Hare with Amber Eyes*

"*Moughalian's book is a work of alchemy—combining the personal, tragic history writ large, and the somehow uplifting power of enduring art.*" —**Elizabeth Taylor,** *National Book Review*

ABOUT THE AUTHOR: **Sato Moughalian** is an award-winning flutist in New York City and Artistic Director of Perspectives Ensemble. Since 2007, Ms. Moughalian has also traveled to Turkey, England, Israel, Palestine, and France to uncover the traces of her grandfather's life and work, has published articles, and gives talks on the genesis of Jerusalem's Armenian ceramic art.

April 2019 | Hardcover | $30.00 | 9781503601932 | Redwood Press

CONVERSATION STARTERS

1. Before reading *Feast of Ashes*, had you heard of the ceramicist David Ohannessian? Were you familiar with the ceramic tile art of Jerusalem?

2. The author relied heavily on her mother's transcriptions of family oral histories to research and write *Feast of Ashes*. Does your own family have a tradition of sharing stories from older generations, or passing stories on to the next generation?

3. What impact did Tavit's family's move from the remote mountain village of Mouradchai to the city of Eskishehir have on his upbringing? Have you had similar experiences, in which moving to a new place or environment opened up new possibilities for you?

4. How did Tavit's job as an assistant to the largest egg merchant and exporter in Eskishehir broaden his exposure to art and culture?

5. During Tavit's years of ceramics training in the late 19th century, tourists commonly visited ateliers to observe artists at work. Have you ever had the opportunity to watch a master artist (e.g., glassblower, woodworker, or painter) create a piece of art? If so, describe your experience.

6. In spite of the ongoing governmental upheavals across Ottoman lands near the turn of the 19th century, how did restoration programs and the new regime affect architecture and the ceramics industry?

7. Why was Tavit and his family exiled from Kutahya after Tavit made the painful decision to renounce his Christian identity and accept Islam?

8. There are many images of tiles panels and ceramics throughout the book. Which one is your favorite, and why?

9. Throughout *Feast of Ashes*, how does Tavit utilize his resourcefulness and relentless drive to keep both his family and the Armenian ceramics tradition alive in Jerusalem and beyond?

10. The author conducted extensive research and traveled far to better understand her family's history. Have you conducted any research of your own to learn more about your family's past?

GOODBYE, MY HAVANA: THE LIFE AND TIMES OF A GRINGA IN REVOLUTIONARY CUBA

Anna Veltfort

Set against a backdrop of world-changing events during the headiest years of the Cuban Revolution, *Goodbye, My Havana* follows Anna Veltfort's young alter ego Connie as her once relatively privileged life among a community of anti-imperialist expatriates turns to progressive disillusionment and heartbreak. The consolidation of Castro's position brings violence, cruelty, and betrayal to Connie's doorstep. And the crackdown that ultimately forces her family and others to flee for their lives includes homosexuals among its targets—Connie's coming-of-age story is one also about the dangers of coming out. Looking back with a mixture of hardheaded clarity and tenderness at her alter ego and a forgotten era, with this gripping graphic memoir Anna Veltfort takes leave of the past even as she brings neglected moments of the Cold War into the present.

"This remarkable and heartfelt book is a loving ode to Cuba, a cautionary tale about the politics of oppression, and proof positive that the personal is always political and the political always personal." —**Justin Hall, editor of** *No Straight Lines: Four Decades of Queer Comics*

"With clear and striking images, Veltfort's insider/outsider view of 1960s Cuba offers a resonant glimpse into an often misunderstood time and place. From moment to moment, readers will find themselves both riveted and wonderfully informed." —**Chantel Acevedo, author of** *The Distant Marvels: A Novel*

"This story of a woman and a nation simultaneously coming of age, their histories inextricably bound together during each of their most formative years, is like no other book I know of." —**Alejandro Velasco, New York University**

ABOUT THE AUTHOR: **Anna Veltfort** is a graphic designer and illustrator who lives in New York.

September 2019 | Paperback | $24.00 | 9781503610491 | Redwood Press

CONVERSATION STARTERS

1. How did Ted's political participation influence Connie as a youth in California? Did your parents' political leanings when you were a child impact your political opinions as an adult?

2. What was life like for Connie in Cuba when she and her family first arrived? Do you get the sense that she enjoyed living there?

3. The Bay of Pigs Invasion and the Cuban Missile Crisis were significant events that took place in Cuba while Connie was in high school. Do you remember the big current events that occurred during your youth? Did they directly affect your day-to-day life?

4. Connie's college experience at the University of Havana was enthralling and, some might say, atypical. For example, she and her professors and peers were called on to help with farm labor, she met interesting people such as Allen Ginsberg, and she interviewed villagers for social research on behalf of the government. What aspect did you find the most fascinating, and why?

5. Life for homosexuals in revolutionary Cuba was very difficult, as many were criminalized or persecuted for their sexual orientation. How did Connie navigate through this hateful environment as a young adult? How did her network of friends help her overcome obstacles?

6. *Goodbye, My Havana* paints a picture of both the political and social landscape in Cuba during the Cuban Revolution. Did you learn anything new about the revolution that you didn't previously know about?

7. In the epilogue, the author writes, "My love for Cuba, my friends there, for the aching beauty of Havana, never wavered, despite Havana's growing decay and the disillusionment that followed, little by little, in the ensuing years." Do you have previous experiences that are nostalgic for you that you think fondly of, even after many years have passed?

THE HELLO GIRLS: AMERICA'S FIRST WOMEN SOLDIERS
Elizabeth Cobbs

In 1918, the U.S. Army Signal Corps sent 223 women to France at General Pershing's explicit request. They were masters of the latest technology: the telephone switchboard. While suffragettes picketed the White House and President Wilson struggled to persuade a segregationist Congress to give women of all races the vote, these courageous young women swore the army oath and settled into their new roles. Elizabeth Cobbs reveals the challenges they faced in a war zone where male soldiers wooed, mocked, and ultimately celebrated them.

The army discharged the last Hello Girls in 1920, the year Congress ratified the Nineteenth Amendment. When they sailed home, they were unexpectedly dismissed without veterans' benefits and began a sixty-year battle that a handful of survivors carried to triumph in 1979.

"What an eye-opener! Cobbs unearths the original letters and diaries of these forgotten heroines and weaves them into a fascinating narrative with energy and zest." —**Cokie Roberts, author of *Capital Dames***

"This engaging history crackles with admiration for the women who served in the U.S. Army Signal Corps during the First World War, becoming the country's first female soldiers." —***New Yorker***

"Utterly delightful ... Cobbs very adroitly weaves the story of the Signal Corps into that larger story of American women fighting for the right to vote, but it's the warm, fascinating job she does bringing her cast ... to life that gives this book its memorable charisma ... This terrific book pays them a long-warranted tribute." —***Christian Science Monitor***

ABOUT THE AUTHOR: **Elizabeth Cobbs** is a historian, *New York Times* bestselling novelist, and documentary filmmaker. She is Melbern G. Glasscock Chair in American History at Texas A&M University and a Research Fellow at Stanford's Hoover Institution. Cobbs is the author of several books on American history and winner of the Allan Nevins Prize.

May 2019 | Paperback | $17.95 | 9780674237438 | Harvard University Press

....

CONVERSATION STARTERS

1. "Yet Wilson drew a line at votes for women, which violated the laws of nature, he thought. Female political activity was both offensive and ludicrous ... he told a colleague that he was 'definitely and irreconcilably opposed to woman suffrage; woman's place was in the home, and the type of woman who took an active part in the suffrage agitation was totally abhorrent to him.'" (11) How and why does Wilson's point of view change throughout his presidency? Why do his opinions change?

2. The Navy enlisted females in March of 1917. The Marines enlisted females in August of 1918. "They and the naval recruits were the first women admitted to full military rank by the United States. Nearly thirteen thousand joined." (60) Why was the Army so unwilling to enlist women? Do you know if the Navy and the Marines are still more forward thinking than the Army today?

3. British Prime Minister David Lloyd George said, "To give the women no voice would be an outrage ... That is why the women question has become largely a war question." (122) Why is it more about war? How does England view the woman's role, and this issue, differently from the US?

4. "Serving in their navy blue skirts, 'upon the very skirts and edges of the battle,' they embodied the claim of the 1848 Seneca Falls Declaration of Sentiments: 'We hold these truths to be self-evident: that all men and women are created equal.'" (304) And yet they were not created or treated equally. Even though the declaration was from almost 100 years prior, why was it so hard for men in the government, the Army, and male citizens in general to accept?

5. On page 307, Cobbs quotes former First Lady Michelle Obama: "It reminds us of stories we hear from our mothers and grandmothers about how... even though they worked so hard, jumped over every hurdle to prove themselves, it was never enough." How has reading this book deepened your understanding of this quote?

6. "Today, females constitute roughly 15 percent of the armed forces. Many aspects of their service seem routine rather than remarkable. Yet their role in combat remains deeply controversial. It challenges our beliefs about what females can or should do." (4) After finishing this book, what new appreciation or questions do you have about how women serve and are treated in the armed services today?

HERE WE ARE: AMERICAN DREAMS, AMERICAN NIGHTMARES
Aarti Namdev Shahani

A heartfelt memoir about the immigrant experience from NPR correspondent Aarti Shahani, *Here We Are: American Dreams, American Nightmares* follows the lives of Aarti, the precocious scholarship kid at one of Manhattan's most elite prep schools, and her dad, the shopkeeper who mistakenly sells watches and calculators to the notorious Cali drug cartel. Together, the two represent the extremes that coexist in our country, even within a single family, and a truth about immigrants that gets lost in the headlines. It isn't a matter of good or evil; it's complicated. *Here We Are* is a coming-of-age story, a love letter from an outspoken modern daughter to her soft-spoken Old World father. She never expected they'd become best friends.

"Aarti Shahani's book is destined to take its place among the finest memoirs written in recent decades—a heartbreaking, hilarious and tender love letter to the millions of people who have made their way across lands and oceans to try and find a new life in America. This book will take you on a vivid, almost cinematic journey that is both beautiful and unforgettable." —**Guy Raz, co-creator of** *How I Built This,* *Wow in the World,* **and** *TED Radio Hour*

"Clear-eyed and compulsively readable, shot through with compassion, humor and heart, Here We Are *is a quintessential immigrant story and an urgent call for change."* —*Shelf Awareness*

ABOUT THE AUTHOR: **Aarti Namdev Shahani** is a correspondent for NPR based in Silicon Valley, covering the largest companies on earth. Before journalism, Shahani was a community organizer in New York City, helping prisoners and families facing deportation. She received a Master's in Public Policy from the Harvard Kennedy School of Government. She was among the youngest recipients of the Charles H. Revson Fellowship at Columbia University and is an alumna of A Better Chance, Inc. Shahani grew up in Flushing, Queens.

October 2019 | Hardcover | $26.99 | 9781250204752 | Celadon Books

CONVERSATION STARTERS

1. Why did Aarti's parents decide to come to America even though they didn't have papers? Do you think they made the right decision?

2. How do you think A Better Chance Inc. and Brearley changed Aarti's perspectives and the course of her life?

3. What were the effects of the September 11, 2001 attacks on Aarti's advocacy efforts in New York and Washington, DC?

4. Aarti describes the gentrification of the area on Broadway where her father and uncle had their store. Have you seen anything similar happening in areas near you?

5. How do you feel about Judge Blumenfeld's criticism to Aarti: "You're not living a life about what you were really born to do"?

6. How did Aarti's relationship with her father evolve over the course of their story? In what ways did the tragedy he experienced actually increase their understanding of one another?

7. Why do you think Aarti became a journalist? How does her work as a journalist inform the way she shared her family's story?

8. Aarti comes to question if the U.S. is her home, and her father's home. What would you say makes your country your home?

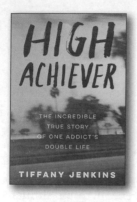

HIGH ACHIEVER: THE INCREDIBLE TRUE STORY OF ONE ADDICT'S DOUBLE LIFE
Tiffany Jenkins

An up-close portrait of the mind of an addict and a life unraveled by narcotics—a memoir of captivating urgency and surprising humor that puts a human face on the opioid crisis.

When word got out that Tiffany Jenkins was withdrawing from opiates on the floor of a jail cell, people in her town were shocked. Not because of the twenty felonies she'd committed, or the nature of her crimes, or even that she'd been captain of the high school cheerleading squad just a few years earlier, but because her boyfriend was a Deputy Sherriff, and his friends—their friends—were the ones who'd arrested her.

A raw and twisty page-turning memoir that reads like fiction, *High Achiever* spans Tiffany's life as an active opioid addict, her 120 days in a Florida jail where every officer despised what she'd done to their brother in blue, and her eventual recovery. With heart-racing urgency and unflinching honesty, Jenkins takes you inside the grips of addiction and the desperate decisions it breeds. She is a born storyteller who lived an incredible story, from blackmail by an ex-boyfriend to a soul-shattering deal with a drug dealer, and her telling brims with suspense and unexpected wit. But the true surprise is her path to recovery. Tiffany breaks through the stigma and silence to offer hope and inspiration to anyone battling the disease—whether it's a loved one or themselves.

"Raw, brutal, and shocking. Move over, Orange Is the New Black.*"*
—**Amy Dresner, author of** *My Fair Junkie*

ABOUT THE AUTHOR: **Tiffany Jenkins** writes about motherhood, addiction, marriage, and life on her blog, Juggling the Jenkins, where she has acquired a huge social media following. She uses her platform to help and inspire others who are struggling with motherhood, mental health, addiction, and those who just need a good laugh. She speaks frequently about addiction and recovery. She lives with her husband and three children in Sarasota, Florida.

June 2019 | Paperback | $15.99 | 9780593135938 | Harmony

CONVERSATION STARTERS

1. Discuss the way Tiffany chooses to tell her story: the reader is immediately thrust into prison, and introduced to her as an inmate before they are introduced to her as a person. What do you think about the chronology of the book?

2. Tiffany weaves humor into the memoir's narrative. Which of her actions and thoughts were most surprising to you? How does her sense of humor impact your reaction to the scenes? Do you feel the humor or sarcasm take away from her experience, or do you think they make it more accessible?

3. Tiffany structures her story so that many of the chapters end in a shocking reveal. Did you find this to be an effective strategy for drawing readers in? What was the most shocking or surprising moment of her story for you?

4. Many people consider addiction to be a family disease. Discuss how Tiffany's drug addiction – and recovery – impacts her closest relationships. How are different family members and loved ones affected?

5. Further to the above, discuss the differences between Tiffany's relationships while abusing drugs versus while sober in prison. She mentions that Sarah, who she met in prison, was one of her first true friends. Discuss her friendship with Kayla. What differences do you see between the women?

6. In Chapter 38, Dr. Peters questions the reality of Tiffany's story. Did you ever feel that she wasn't being completely honest? Or did you find her to be a reliable narrator? Discuss how your reactions to her story shifted over the course of the book.

7. The book ends with Tiffany sharing her story with a group of recovering addicts, many whose stories are much like her own. What do you think about her second chance at life, and how she has chosen to share her message? If you got the chance to ask Tiffany one question, what would it be?

8. Did Tiffany's story about the tumultuous nature of addiction change any preconceptions that you might have had about drug abuse or the opioid crisis in the U.S.? Do you feel more empathetic or more distanced from those in similar situations to Tiffany's after reading her story?

THE MISSING PAGES: THE MODERN LIFE OF A MEDIEVAL MANUSCRIPT, FROM GENOCIDE TO JUSTICE

Heghnar Zeitlian Watenpaugh

In 2010, the world's wealthiest art institution, the J. Paul Getty Museum, found itself confronted by a century-old genocide. The Armenian Church was suing for the return of eight pages from the Zeytun Gospels, a manuscript illuminated by the greatest medieval Armenian artist, Toros Roslin. Protected for centuries in a remote church, the holy manuscript had followed the waves of displaced people exterminated during the Armenian genocide. Passed from hand to hand, caught in the confusion and brutality of the First World War, it was cleaved in two. Decades later, the manuscript found its way to the Republic of Armenia, while its missing eight pages came to the Getty.

The Missing Pages is the biography of a manuscript that is at once art, sacred object, and cultural heritage. Its tale mirrors the story of its scattered community as Armenians have struggled to redefine themselves after genocide and in the absence of a homeland. Heghnar Zeitlian Watenpaugh follows in the manuscript's footsteps through seven centuries, from medieval Armenia to the killing fields of 1915 Anatolia, the refugee camps of Aleppo, Ellis Island, and Soviet Armenia, and ultimately to a Los Angeles courtroom.

Reconstructing the path of the pages, Watenpaugh uncovers the rich tapestry of an extraordinary artwork and the people touched by it. At once a story of genocide and survival, of unimaginable loss and resilience, *The Missing Pages* captures the human costs of war and persuasively makes the case for a human right to art.

"What makes The Missing Pages *truly remarkable is her gift of storytelling. This is a book with the soul of language—moving, affirming, illuminating."*
—**Mark Arax, author of** *The Dreamt Land: Chasing Dust and Water Across California*

ABOUT THE AUTHOR: **Heghnar Zeitlian Watenpaugh** is Professor of Art History at the University of California, Davis. She is the award-winning author of *The Image of an Ottoman City: Architecture in Aleppo* (2004).

February 2019 | Hardcover | $30.00 | 9780804790444 | Stanford University Press

....

CONVERSATION STARTERS

1. Before you read *The Missing Pages*, were you familiar with illuminated manuscripts? What did you learn about this form of art? What did you learn about Toros Roslin, the miniaturist who worked on the Zeytun Gospels?

2. How does the separation of the Canon Tables from its mother manuscript, the Zeytun Gospels, mirror or symbolize the history of the Armenian people?

3. The lawsuit against the J. Paul Getty Museum incited a dispute on who has rightful ownership to the Canon Tables, which have tremendous artistic and historical importance. What are your thoughts on which group should own the Canon Tables? Can you think of other examples in history that have spurred discussion on the issue of rightful ownership?

4. Material objects can hold cultural and religious importance to its owners, especially for survivors of war and genocide. Do you or your family have any significant objects that would be difficult to part with if they were lost, stolen, or destroyed?

5. The author tells the biography of the Zeytun Gospels via its global travels throughout history. Which geographical stop of the manuscript's journey did you find the most intriguing, and why?

6. Discuss the importance of the lawsuit taking place in Los Angeles, and the response of the Armenian community to the settlement.

7. How will the five-year-long lawsuit involving the Canon Tables, and the settlement reached by both parties, help shape the history of the Armenian genocide?

8. Exhibitions at renowned art museums like the Getty Museum tell innovative stories about its objects on display, communicating scholarly research to the public. Has reading *The Missing Pages* influenced the way you will observe art and historical objects at museums in the future?

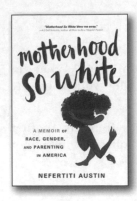

MOTHERHOOD SO WHITE: A MEMOIR OF RACE, GENDER, AND PARENTING IN AMERICA

Nefertiti Austin

What's it like to be a Black mother in a world where the face of motherhood is overwhelmingly white?

That's the question Nefertiti, a single African American woman, faced when she decided she wanted to adopt a Black baby boy out of the foster care system. Eager to finally join the motherhood ranks, Nefertiti was shocked when people started asking her why she wanted to adopt a "crack baby" or said that she would never be able to raise a Black son on her own. She realized that American society saw motherhood through a white lens, and that there would be no easy understanding or acceptance of the kind of family she hoped to build.

Motherhood So White is the story of Nefertiti's fight to create the family she always knew she was meant to have and the story of motherhood that all American families need now. In this unflinching account of her parenting journey, Nefertiti examines the history of adoption in the African American community, faces off against stereotypes of single, Black motherhood, and confronts the reality of raising children of color in racially charged, modern-day America.

"A sharp reminder that in our society, parenting is not a colorblind experience." —KJ Dell'Antonia, author of *How to Be a Happier Parent*

"A needed and important contribution." —Meg Lemke, Editor-in-Chief of *MUTHA*

ABOUT THE AUTHOR: **Nefertiti Austin** writes about the erasure of diverse voices in motherhood. Her work around this topic has been short-listed for literary awards and appeared in the *Huffington Post*, HuffPost Live, and *The Atlantic*. Nefertiti's expertise stems from firsthand experience and degrees in U.S. history and African American studies.

September 2019 | Hardcover | 304 pp | $25.99 | 9781492679011 | Sourcebooks

CONVERSATION STARTERS

1. Describe Nefertiti's relationship with her parents, Diane and Harold, and her grandparents, Ann and Henry. How do you think these relationships formed Nefertiti's first views on parenthood and what it means to be a parent?

2. How did your own upbringing influence your take on what it means to be a parent? What are some of the lessons you've learned through your childhood experiences that influenced how you do, or would, parent today?

3. What is Nefertiti's experience with "Black adoption," and how did it impact her choices later in life?

4. Nefertiti describes how, suddenly, the stirrings of motherhood turned into an overwhelming desire to pursue becoming a parent. If you are a parent, what moved you to make that decision? Which path to parenthood did you choose?

5. Put yourself in Nefertiti's shoes—if you were telling your family and friends that you've decided to adopt a Black son from the foster care system, how do you think they would react? Were you surprised by the stereotypes and prejudices Nefertiti faced both within and outside her own community? Speak on what you imagine that experience was like for her.

6. What are some of the stereotypes and fears Nefertiti had to confront while raising August in today's racially charged America? What about with Cherish? What were some of the biases Nefertiti personally faced as a single Black mother?

7. *Motherhood So White* showcases many of the conversations and experiences parents of Black children face—from teaching their children about unconscious bias to explaining the traps embedded in our current cultural landscape. Speak about those conversations. Were there any that surprised you? Any that you, in your own experiences of parenthood, have or haven't had with your own children?

999: THE EXTRAORDINARY YOUNG WOMEN OF THE FIRST OFFICIAL JEWISH TRANSPORT TO AUSCHWITZ

Heather Dune Macadam

From National Book Award nominee Heather Dune Macadam, the untold story of the 999 young, unmarried Jewish women who were tricked on March 25, 1942 into boarding the train that became the first official transport to Auschwitz. Timed to coincide with the 75th anniversary of the liberation of Auschwitz and drawing on extensive interviews with survivors, historians, witnesses, and relatives of those first deportees, *999* is an important addition to Holocaust literature and women's history.

On March 25, 1942, nearly a thousand young, unmarried Jewish women boarded a train in Poprad, Slovakia. Believing they were going to work in a factory for a few months, they were eager to report for government service. Instead, the young women—many of them teenagers—were sent to Auschwitz. Their government paid 500 Reich Marks (about $200) apiece for the Nazis to take them as slave labor. Of those 999 innocent deportees, only a few would survive.

The facts of the first official Jewish transport to Auschwitz are little known, yet profoundly relevant today. These were not resistance fighters or prisoners of war. There were no men among them. Sent to almost certain death, the young women were powerless and insignificant not only because they were Jewish—but also because they were female.

ABOUT THE AUTHOR: **Heather Dune Macadam** is the National Book Award-nominated author of *Rena's Promise: A Story of Sisters in Auschwitz*, which was also nominated for the Christopher Award, the American Jewish Award, and the National Library Association Award. A board member of the Cities of Peace: Auschwitz and the director and president of the Rena's Promise Foundation, her work in the battle against Holocaust denial have been recognized by Yad Vashem in the UK and Israel, the USC Shoah Foundation, the National Museum of Jewish History in Bratislava, Slovakia, and the Panstowe Museum of Auschwitz in Oswiecim, Poland. She divides her time between New York and Herefordshire, England.

December 2019 | Hardcover | $28.00 | 9780806539362 | Citadel Press

CONVERSATION STARTERS

1. How does the author's research bring the reader into the immediacy of the looming horrors of The Holocaust? How does the author paint a picture not just of being a Jew during the War, but of being a woman?

2. Macadam, along with several families, retraced the girls' journey to Auschwitz and then on to Birkenau. How did that experience inform her descriptions of their passage? How did she use that first-hand information to make it more immediate for you?

3. In reading about the Nazis' government-mandated separations, deportations, and resettlements of Jewish people, how did you feel reading the book about these separations? What did you think about when people had their belongings taken away, then their children?

4. Much of the book's tragedy comes from the deep loss of their tight-knit community – the collective loss of their loved ones and neighbors, how and why they are targeted by the law, how they are lied to, the coded messages their daughters send to them. How do these horrors make you think about your own life?

5. 999 reviews how the government justified its actions, how the press disseminated falsehoods about the Jews resettlements with fake pictures, misleading headlines, and manipulative articles. How does this make you think about "fake news"?

6. One of the ways the sisters survive is by securing "decent work," not manual labor, that would protect them from potential accidental and mortal hazards, and improve their physical conditions, but it could not save those you loved. How does this revise your view of the work, of the power you have over your own life?

7. 999 describes how the strong survive and the weak are exterminated. Today the weak are tended to in order to grow strong again. What kinds of emotions do you feel upon reading of this reversal of humanity – dread, pity, horror, shock, disbelief?

8. The book highlights the entwined lives of two sisters and their friend. Which one of the three women's stories did you find most compelling, and why?

PRINCESS OF THE HITHER ISLES: A BLACK SUFFRAGIST'S STORY FROM THE JIM CROW SOUTH

Adele Logan Alexander

A compelling reconstruction of the life of a black suffragist

Born during the Civil War into a slave-holding family that included black, white, and Cherokee forebears, Adella Hunt Logan dedicated herself to advancing political and educational opportunities for the African American community. She taught at Alabama's Tuskegee Institute, but also joined the segregated woman suffrage movement, passing for white in order to fight for the rights of people of color. Her determination—as a wife, mother, scholar, and activist—to challenge the draconian restraints of race and gender generated conflicts that precipitated her tragic demise.

Historian Adele Logan Alexander—Adella's granddaughter—bridges the chasms that frustrate efforts to document the lives of those who traditionally have been silenced, weaving together family lore, historical research, and literary imagination into a riveting, multi-generational family saga.

"There is a beauty in reading Adele Logan Alexander's epic biography of her grandmother that comes with knowing it is, for her, a devotional act, not to romanticize the past but to set out fearlessly to unearth—and touch—its very heart. Alexander's Princess of the Hither Isles *is both a definitive rendering of a life and a remarkable study of the interplay of race and gender in an America whose shadows still haunt us today."* —**Henry Louis Gates, Jr.**

"If you combine the pleasures of a seductive novel, discovering a real American heroine, and learning the multiracial history of this country that wasn't in our textbooks, you will have an idea of the great gift that Adele Logan Alexander has given us in Princess of the Hither Isles. *By writing about her own grandmother, she helps us discover our own country."* —**Gloria Steinem**

ABOUT THE AUTHOR: **Adele Logan Alexander** taught for many years at George Washington University. She is the author of *Ambiguous Lives: Free Women of Color in Rural Georgia* among other books.

September 2019 | Hardcover | $30.00 | 9780300242607 | Yale University Press

CONVERSATION STARTERS

1. The author employs a blend of deep historical research, family lore, and literary imagination to bring her grandmother, Adella, to life. What do you think of this genre-defying approach?

2. What do Adella's experiences suggest about the importance, efficacy, and possible pitfalls of interracial relationships?

3. Discuss the importance of family as a determining factor in Adella's world and in the black community.

4. In the context of contemporary thinking and parlance, discuss whether Adella Hunt Logan should be characterized as a black feminist.

5. Adella's life includes both extraordinary achievement and significant tragedy. How does she cope with loss and stress at various stages of her life?

6. Even though they have many privileges, Adella and her family face racial discrimination in all aspects of their lives. What has changed? What has stayed the same?

7. Adella endures two risky and unwanted pregnancies following a dangerous procedure. How does this experience impact her views on women's right to control their own bodies? How does the requirement that her husband provide permission for her medical procedure affect Adella's thinking?

8. The book includes instances when Adella passes as white, as well as occasions when she corrects people who misidentify her as a white woman. Discuss the ways Adella and her mixed-race family navigate the complex racial landscape. Does passing for white constitute a moral betrayal of the African American community?

9. The biases of prominent activists of her time disappoint Adella on several occasions. Both Susan B. Anthony's racism and Booker T. Washington's sexism frustrate her. How does Adella handle these situations? How might she handle them differently today?

10. Instances of sexual abuse by powerful men appear throughout the book. Discuss the ways sexual misconduct and violence are handled in Adella's world. How do racial factors play an exacerbating role with respect to such abuse? Have things changed? How?

REBEL POET: MORE STORIES FROM A 21ST CENTURY INDIAN
Louis V. Clark III (Two Shoes)

Louis V. Clark III (Two Shoes) takes an honest, humorous, and at times heartbreaking look—in poetry and prose—of the complexities of being Indian today in this much anticipated follow-up to his breakout memoir *How to Be an Indian in the 21st Century*. He delves more deeply into the themes of family, community, grief, and the struggle to make a place in the world when your very identity is considered suspect.

ABOUT THE AUTHOR: Born and raised on the Oneida Reservation, **Louis V. Clark III (Two Shoes)** turned to poetry to continue the oral tradition of his people, the People of the Standing Stone. His memoir *How to Be an Indian in the 21st Century*, published by the Wisconsin Historical Society Press, received the Midwest Booksellers Choice Award for 2017.

August 2019 | Paperback | $15.95 | 9780870209291 | Wisconsin Historical Society Press

CONVERSATION STARTERS

1. The book opens with an Oneida Indian prayer of Thanksgiving. How does this set the stage of Louis's identity discussions that follow?

2. What inspired Louis to write poetry? What are some things that would inspire you to write poetry?

3. What challenges did Louis face as a child related to his struggles with identity?

4. What kind of discrimination has Louis faced? How does he channel his encounters with racism into his poetry?

5. As Louis writes in "I-A Poet," he identifies with and copes with his two worlds – Polish and Oneida Indian. In what ways do you cope with living in two (culturally, racially, personally, etc.) different worlds?

6. Louis writes about the more hidden forms of racism he encountered at work, being held back from positions and promotions, etc. Have you encountered this? Have you seen this done to others? Will his discussion of covert racism affect the way you view your workplace; if so, how?

7. What particular poem stood out to you and why?

8. How do our multiple identities shape the way we see the world? How do you see this reflected in *Rebel Poet*?

9. How does the content of the poems evolve throughout the book?

10. What makes Louis' poetry stand out from other poets?

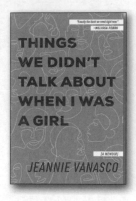

THINGS WE DIDN'T TALK ABOUT WHEN I WAS A GIRL: A MEMOIR
Jeannie Vanasco

Jeannie Vanasco has had the same nightmare since she was a teenager. She startles awake, saying his name. It is always about him: one of her closest high school friends, a boy named Mark. A boy who raped her.

When her nightmares worsen, Jeannie decides after fourteen years of silence to reach out to Mark. He agrees to talk on the record and meet in person. "It's the least I can do," he says.

Jeannie details her friendship with Mark before and after the assault, asking the brave and urgent question: Is it possible for a good person to commit a terrible act? Jeannie interviews Mark, exploring how rape has impacted his life as well as her own. She examines the language surrounding sexual assault and pushes against its confines, contributing to and deepening the #MeToo discussion.

Exacting and courageous, *Things We Didn't Talk About When I Was a Girl* is part memoir, part true crime record, and part testament to the strength of female friendships a recounting and reckoning that will inspire us to ask harder questions and interrogate our biases. Jeannie Vanasco examines and dismantles long-held myths of victimhood, discovering grace and power in this genre-bending investigation into the trauma of sexual violence.

"Exactly the book we need right now." —**Melissa Febos**

ABOUT THE AUTHOR: **Jeannie Vanasco** is the author of *The Glass Eye*. Featured by *Poets & Writers* as one of the five best literary nonfiction debuts of 2017, *The Glass Eye* was also selected as a Barnes & Noble Discover Great New Writers Pick, an Indies Introduce Pick, and an Indie Next Pick.

October 2019 | Hardcover | $24.95 | 9781947793453 | Tin House Books

CONVERSATION STARTERS

1. What do you think of the title *Things We Didn't Talk About When I Was a Girl*? Why do you think it is that we don't discuss many of the issues raised in the book? Do you think things have changed at all since you were a kid?

2. Jeannie Vanasco's memoir dovetails with many concerns raised by the #MeToo movement. Did you find you were reading her memoir in the context of this movement?

3. How do you feel about Vanasco including Mark's perspective in the narrative? Did your feelings about his inclusion change as you read?

4. Vanasco worries that readers might think her conversations with Mark are a "performance of gender" or that she spends too much time humanizing him. Did you have these feelings?

5. Outside of the interviews with Mark, Vanasco's partner, Chris, offers a male viewpoint. How might the book have been different if not for Chris' perspective?

6. Vanasco's female friends play an important role in the narrative. What do you think this memoir might generate in terms of conversations amongst women? Did you talk to your female friends about this book?

7. Many of the college students Vanasco teaches have experienced sexual assault. Do you think this book would benefit readers in their teens and early twenties?

8. Vanasco's first memoir, *The Glass Eye*, deals with issues of mental illness. In *Things We Didn't Talk About When I Was a Girl*, Vanasco states that this fact might make readers worry that she is an unreliable narrator. Did you have this concern while reading?

9. Vanasco struggles to define what happened to her as rape, but ultimately decides to use the word rape. Do you think that this decision represents an important moment in the memoir? Do you think there is a strong difference between the terms "sexual assault" and "rape"?

10. Throughout the book, transcripts of Vanasco's conversations with Mark are interspersed between sections of reflection, memory, research, and more. How did this construction influence your reading of the book? What did it mean to you to be able to read the transcripts directly?

WHAT GOD IS HONORED HERE?: WRITINGS ON MISCARRIAGE AND INFANT LOSS BY AND FOR NATIVE WOMEN AND WOMEN OF COLOR

Edited by Shannon Gibney and Kao Kalia Yang

What God Is Honored Here? is the first book of its kind—and urgently necessary. This is a literary collection of voices of Indigenous women and women of color who have undergone miscarriage and infant loss, experiences that disproportionately affect women who have often been cast toward the margins in the United States of America.

In its heartbreaking beauty, this book offers an integral perspective on how culture and religion, spirit and body, unite in the reproductive lives of women of color and Indigenous women as they bear witness to loss, search for what is not there, and claim for themselves and others their fundamental humanity. Powerfully and with brutal honesty, they write about what it means to reclaim life in the face of death.

"Pregnancy loss is a most enigmatic human sorrow, unique to every woman who suffers it. These stories of resilience, grief, and restoration are essential, for to understand is to heal." —**Louise Erdrich**

"What God Is Honored Here? is the hardest and most important book I've read about parenting, loss, and imagination. It's also the most frightening book in my world, but not because it is horrific: it is about the terrifying possibilities of love." —**Kiese Laymon, author of** *Heavy*

"These writers have created a sacred space, a temple, in which the unspeakable can be shared. A book of astounding grace and strength." —**Thi Bui, author of** *The Best We Could Do*

ABOUT THE EDITORS: **Shannon Gibney** is a writer, educator, activist, and the author of two YA novels: *See No Color*, which won the Minnesota Book Award in Young People's Literature, and *Dream Country*. **Kao Kalia Yang** is author of *The Latehomecomer*, winner of two Minnesota Book Awards and a finalist for two national awards, and *The Song Poet*, winner of a Minnesota Book Award and a finalist for several national awards.

October 2019 | Paperback | $19.95 | 9781517907938 | University of Minnesota Press

CONVERSATION STARTERS

1. What is the significance of the title of the collection? What do you think the space of "here" refers to for the women in this anthology?

2. How does this book speak to the times we are living in and the conditions and realities of the lives of Native Women and Women of Color?

3. What are the advantages of putting together a collection of voices as opposed to these women individually writing and publishing their individual stories? What are the disadvantages?

4. This book sheds light on a tragic reality in America: miscarriage and infant loss disproportionately affect Women of Color and Native Women in this country. What can we do to alleviate and/or address this problem?

5. If you had to choose one piece from this book to speak to the collection as a whole, which story or poem would you choose and why?

6. In this collection, we see women from a wide margin of society contending with pregnancy loss and infant death. What is the role of your religion, culture, and/or beliefs in guiding your response to these stories?

7. Is it possible to heal from the traumas of pregnancy loss and infant death?

8. Have the experiences of miscarriage and infant loss impacted your own life and altered your stories? How?

9. How do the men in your life deal with miscarriage and infant loss? What does this reveal about the different ways our societies and cultures treat men and women in these situations? What about individuals who are gender queer?

10. How does this collection speak to the power of love in women's lives?

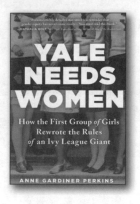

YALE NEEDS WOMEN: HOW THE FIRST GROUP OF GIRLS REWROTE THE RULES OF AN IVY LEAGUE GIANT

Anne Gardiner Perkins

In the summer of 1969, Yale University, the Ivy League institution dedicated to graduating "one thousand male leaders" each year finally decided to open its doors to the nation's top female students. The landmark decision was a huge step forward for women's equality in education.

Or was it?

The experience the first undergraduate women found when they stepped onto Yale's imposing campus was not the same one their male peers enjoyed. Isolated from one another, singled out as oddities and sexual objects, and barred from many of the privileges an elite education was supposed to offer, many of the first girls found themselves immersed in an overwhelmingly male culture they were unprepared to face.

Yale Needs Women is the story of how these young women fought against the backward-leaning traditions of a centuries-old institution and created the opportunities that would carry them into the future. Anne Gardiner Perkins's unflinching account of a group of young women striving for change is an inspiring story of strength, resilience, and courage that continues to resonate today.

"Perkins' richly detailed narrative is a reminder that gender equality has never come easy, but instead borne from the exertions of those who precede us. You must read this book." —**Nathalia Holt,** *New York Times* **bestselling author of** *Rise of the Rocket Girls*

"Yale Needs Women is an important addition to feminist history." —**Henry Louis Gates, Jr., Alphonse Fletcher University Professor, Harvard University, and host of PBS's** *Finding*

ABOUT THE AUTHOR: **Anne Gardiner Perkins** is a graduate of Yale University (BA, American history, 1981), and was elected the first woman editor-in-chief of the *Yale Daily News*. She lives in Boston.

September 2019 | Hardcover | $25.99 | 9781492687740 | Sourcebooks

CONVERSATION STARTERS

1. After screening for academic strength, Sam Chauncey and Elga Wasserman looked for toughness when selecting Yale's first women undergraduates. "There was no point in taking a timid woman and putting her in this environment," said Chauncey, "because it could crush you." Do you think they were right to consider a student's toughness? As a high school senior, would you have met this standard?

2. *Yale Needs Women* focuses in particular on the experiences of five women students—Shirley Daniels, Kit McClure, Lawrie Mifflin, Connie Royster, and Betty Spahn. With which of these five did you identify most closely? Why? Was there another character with which you connected more strongly?

3. Yale may have gone coed in 1969, yet women—whether student, administrator, or professor—were still barred from many of the traditional paths to influence and power, both at Yale and beyond. Can you provide some examples? How did women create power in other ways?

4. What parallels do you see between the experiences and activism of black and white women students at Yale? What are the differences?

5. *Yale Needs Women* includes a center section of photographs. Choose one and discuss how you first responded to it. What drew you to this photo in particular? What questions, if any, do you still have about it?

6. Yale's first women undergraduates sometimes found themselves the only woman in a classroom full of men. Were you ever the only person of your gender in the room? How did it affect how you behaved? How others behaved towards you? Compare this to a situation in which your gender was in the majority.

7. *Yale Needs Women* chronicles some of the sexual assault and harassment suffered by Yale's women students. How has this situation improved for women college students since 1969? How has it remained the same?

YOUNG ADULT

THE ASSASSINATION OF BRANGWAIN SPURGE

M.T. Anderson and Eugene Yelchin

A National Book Award Finalist, *New York Times* Editors' Choice, and Junior Library Guild Selection

Subverting convention, award-winning creators M. T. Anderson and Eugene Yelchin pair up for an anarchic, outlandish, and deeply political saga of warring elf and goblin kingdoms.

Uptight elfin historian Brangwain Spurge is on a mission: survive being catapulted across the mountains into goblin territory, deliver a priceless peace offering to their mysterious dark lord, and spy on the goblin kingdom — from which no elf has returned alive in more than a hundred years. Brangwain's host, the goblin archivist Werfel, is delighted to show Brangwain around. They should be the best of friends, but a series of extraordinary double crosses, blunders, and cultural misunderstandings throws these two bumbling scholars into the middle of an international crisis that may spell death for them — and war for their nations. Witty mixed media illustrations show Brangwain's furtive missives back to the elf kingdom, while Werfel's determinedly unbiased narrative tells an entirely different story. A hilarious and biting social commentary that could only come from the likes of National Book Award winner M. T. Anderson and Newbery Honoree Eugene Yelchin, this tale is rife with thrilling action and visual humor ... and a comic disparity that suggests the ultimate victor in a war is perhaps not who won the battles, but who gets to write the history.

"Both moving and hilarious." —***The New York Times Book Review***

"Biting and hysterical, Brangwain and Werfel's adventure is one for the history books." —***Booklist*** (**Starred Review**)

ABOUT THE AUTHORS: **M. T. Anderson** is the author of *Feed*, winner of the Los Angeles Times Book Prize; the National Book Award–winning *The Astonishing Life of Octavian Nothing, Traitor to the Nation, Volume I: The Pox Party* and its sequel, *The Kingdom on the Waves*, both *New York Times* bestsellers and Michael L. Printz Honor Books. **Eugene Yelchin** is a Russian-American author and illustrator of many books for children, including *Breaking Stalin's Nose*, a Newbery Honor Book and *The Rooster Prince of Breslov*, a National Jewish Book Award winner.

September 2018 | Hardcover | $24.99 | 9780763698225 | Candlewick Press
April 2020 | Paperback | 14.99 | 9781536213096 | Candlewick Press

....

CONVERSATION STARTERS

1. There are many ways to tell a story, as *The Assassination of Brangwain Spurge* makes clear. Who are the narrators of this novel? What does each contribute to the story? Which narrator do you find to be the most trustworthy? Why?

2. Take a closer look at Spurge's transmissions back to Elfland. According to Clivers, they depict "whatever he pictures in his mind," his impression of things as opposed to reality. (160) If Spurge were using a camera, how would his transmissions be different? Would they be more honest? Why?

3. For the goblins, "hospitality was holy." (29) What risks does Werfel take to be a good host to Spurge? Why does Spurge mistreat his host? When does he stop acting like a bad guest and start behaving like a good friend? How does that transformation save his life, and Werfel's, too?

4. Books that depict warfare, treachery, and personal humiliation tend not to be very funny, but this one is often hilarious. What is your favorite piece of comic dialogue? What is your favorite comic scene? Why?

5. "Werfel thought of the old saying: *Elf and goblin, we all have pointy ears. So true.*" (81) Beyond their ears, what other characteristics do elves and goblins share? What qualities set them apart?

6. Despite mounting evidence of the rot in his homeland, Spurge is blind to Elfland's problems through most of this novel. Yet Werfel clearly sees the corruption in the goblin kingdom. Why is one scholar more open to disturbing truths about his country than the other?

7. Military strength is highly prized in most nations, but what about intellectual strength? How do ideas and values contribute to a country's security? How do Werfel and Spurge prove the potency of brain power?

8. Perhaps you've heard the assertion "History is written by the victors" in a classroom or on television. What do you think it really means? Does it apply to this novel? Why?

BECOMING BEATRIZ
Tami Charles

It's Beatriz's *quinceañera*, and she is ready to be treated like royalty. But when her brother, the leader of the Diablos, is gunned down by a rival gang, Beatriz will never be the same again. Her dreams of dancing, her hopes for fame, and her love of music died with Junito.

But when handsome brainiac, Nasser, asks her to join a dance competition with him—one that could land them both a role on Beatriz's favorite TV show, *Fame*—Beatriz starts to feel the music again. And Nasser makes her feel alive again. But with her Mami practically catatonic with grief, and her duties with Junito's gang, Beatriz's dreams are put on hold.

Set in 1984, the music, the dancing, and the rhythm of the life of a Puerto Rican teenager in Newark, New Jersey, reveal a story of hope and perseverance. By the time Beatriz turns sixteen, she has a much better idea about what her dreams are made of, what she'll do to achieve them, and how to live the life she wants, rather than a life that someone else decided for her.

"… a necessary portrayal of a young Afro Latina woman who makes her own path." —*Kirkus Reviews* (**Starred Review**)

ABOUT THE AUTHOR: **Tami Charles** is a former teacher and full-time author of picture books, middle grade and young adult novels, and nonfiction. As a teacher, she made it her mission to introduce her students to all types of literature, but especially diverse books. While it was refreshing to see a better selection than what she was accustomed to as a child, Tami felt there weren't nearly as many diverse books as she'd hoped for. It was then that she decided to reignite her passion for writing.

September 2019 | Hardcover | $17.99 | 9781580897785 | Charlesbridge Teen

CONVERSATION STARTERS

1. "Un secreto entre de dos, se quede entre los dos. Pero un secreto entre de tres, sabe todo el mundo." "A secret between two can stay secret—but a secret between three, the whole world knows." What do you think of this saying? Is it possible for more than two people to share a secret? Why or why not?

2. Discuss Junito's secret. Given the historic and cultural setting, what would happen if his secret was revealed?

3. Beatriz is certainly attracted to Nasser, but what else does he represent to her?

4. When truths begin to reveal themselves to Beatriz, her world shatters a little bit. But she still has dance. Would you call that an escape or a destination?

5. Throughout this book, faux newspaper articles are reproduced in the pages, giving a media perspective on the events of Beatriz's life. What do you notice about the tone, format, and scope of these articles? How do they paint a different or similar portrait of Beatriz's life compared to her own words?

6. Each flashback scene is formatted like a track in a music album (Track Five: Dance of the Rumba, December 8, 1983, for example). What does this say about the relationship between music, memory, and history?

7. Writing is an important part of Mami's healing process. What do you think of the difference between her poems and Beatriz's poems? Is there anything about Mami's writing that surprises you? Why or why not?

8. *Becoming Beatriz* opens with a violent episode. What do you think about how this sets the tone and pace of the story?

9. Why does Beatriz refuse to tell the police about what happened with Junito and the Macoutes?

10. "Two feelings break out in a war—hate and loyalty. And honestly, I can't shake either." Discuss this phrase: What is Beatriz's mindset when she thinks it? How does it resonate with your own life?

11. Discuss Beatriz's adult role models. Does she have strong relationships with them? Why does Beatriz resist connection with the adults in her life?

I CAN MAKE THIS PROMISE
Christine Day

All her life, Edie has known that her mom was adopted by a white couple. So, no matter how curious she might be about her Native American heritage, Edie is sure her family doesn't have any answers.

Until the day when she and her friends discover a box hidden in the attic—a box full of letters signed "Love, Edith," and photos of a woman who looks just like her.

Suddenly, Edie has a flurry of new questions about this woman who shares her name. Could she belong to the Native family that Edie never knew about? But if her mom and dad have kept this secret from her all her life, how can she trust them to tell her the truth now?

"Day's novel brings an accessible, much-needed perspective about the very real consequences of Indigenous children being taken from their families and Native Nations. The absence of one's tribal community, loss of culture and lack of connection to relatives have ripple effects for generations." —**Traci Sorell (Cherokee Nation), award-winning author of** *We Are Grateful: Otsaliheliga*

ABOUT THE AUTHOR: **Christine Day** (Upper Skagit) holds a master's degree from the University of Washington, where she created a thesis on Coast Salish weaving traditions. *I Can Make This Promise* is her first novel. Christine lives in the Pacific Northwest with her husband.

October 2019 | Hardcover | $16.99 | 9780062871992 | HarperCollins Children's Books

CONVERSATION STARTERS

1. After finding the box in the attic, Edie asks her parents, "Why am I Edith?" and "Where did my name come from?" (49) What is the story behind Edie's name? By the end of the book, how does she feel about her name?

2. In one of her letters, Edith Graham writes: "I must admit, I'm homesick. It's lonely being the only Indian woman around." (143) Do other characters feel lonely throughout this book? Can you identify any patterns or similarities between their moments of loneliness?

3. Over the course of this novel, Edie's friendships change. Take a moment to reflect on her relationships with Amelia, Serenity, Libby, and Roger. What is the nature of Edie's relationship with each person? How are these characters significant to Edie's growth?

4. Who is Bruno? How does Bruno's journey change and evolve alongside Edie's? Are there any connections between his story and Edith Graham's? Are there connections between Bruno and Edie's mom?

5. How does Edie's identity as an artist change over the course of the book? What are her main sources of inspiration? Do you think her artwork is influenced by her identity as a biracial Native (Duwamish/Suquamish) girl?

6. What is the Indian Child Welfare Act of 1978? Why is this piece of legislation so vital to tribal nations, families, and communities?

7. Why do you think the author chose the title: *I Can Make This Promise?* What is the main promise Edie makes in this story? How does she fulfill this promise in the book? How might she honor it in the future?

8. Make your own promise. Reflect on the people, places, memories, and experiences that are most important to you. What can you do to fulfill this promise right now? How might you honor your promise in the future?

I'M NOT DYING WITH YOU TONIGHT

Kimberly Jones and Gilly Segal

Lena and Campbell aren't friends.

Lena has her killer style, her awesome boyfriend, and a plan. She knows she's going to make it big. Campbell, on the other hand, is just trying to keep her head down and get through the year at her new school.

When both girls attend the Friday night football game, what neither expects is for everything to descend into sudden mass chaos. Chaos born from violence and hate. Chaos that unexpectedly throws them together.

They aren't friends. They hardly understand the other's point of view. But none of that matters when the city is up in flames, and they only have each other to rely on if they're going to survive the night.

"A compelling and powerful novel that is sure to make an impact." —**Angie Thomas**, #1 *New York Times* bestselling author of *The Hate U Give*

"A vital addition to the YA race relations canon." —**Nic Stone**, *New York Times* bestselling author of *Dear Martin*

"A powerful examination of privilege, and how friends are often found in surprising places. Jones and Segal have penned a page-turning debut, as timely as it is addictive." —**David Arnold**, *New York Times* bestselling author of *Mosquitoland* and *Kids of Appetite*

ABOUT THE AUTHORS: **Kimberly Jones** is the former manager of the bookstore Little Shop of Stories and currently works in the entertainment industry. **Gilly Segal** spent her college years in Israel and served in the Israel Defense Forces (IDF). She is currently a lawyer for an advertising agency. Both authors live in Atlanta, Georgia.

August 2019 | Hardcover | $17.99 | 9781492678892 | Sourcebooks Fire

CONVERSATION STARTERS

1. Do you feel that either or both Lena and Campbell begin with a "me vs. you" or "us vs. them" mentality? If so, does that change over the course of the night and why or why not? Do Lena and Campbell ever become an "us"?

2. How do the girls perceive each other upon first meeting? Do they idealize or stereotype one another?

3. What is the racial epithet that starts the fight at the high school? How do each of the characters perceive it?

4. Would the events of this night have transpired the same way if one or both of these characters had been male or male presenting? What might have changed?

5. What do you make of the scene when Lena and Campbell come upon the parking lot full of police? How might their life experiences leading up to that moment create their attitudes?

6. How does Lena's familiarity with the neighborhood drive her decisions when she realizes it is not safe to remain at school during the fight? How does she use her instincts to judge decisions?

7. How does Lena feel about the rivalry between her high school, McPherson, and Jonesville High? What does she think about the racist incidents that occur in the lead up to the football game?

8. How would you characterize Campbell's relationship with her mother and her father? How does that impact her actions during the night of the riot?

9. Does Campbell's attitude toward the police evolve over the course of the novel? If so, how?

10. Lena says Campbell hasn't tried to get to know the neighborhood and walks around like she doesn't live there. What do you think she means by that? What does Campbell realize about herself, if anything, in that conversation?

11. What do you think happens the day after the riot to Campbell and Lena? To the school? To the city?

12. If you could meet one of these characters in real life, what would you say to them?

IN THE NEIGHBORHOOD OF TRUE

Susan Kaplan Carlton

After her father's death, Ruth Robb and her family transplant themselves in the summer of 1958 from New York City to Atlanta. In her new hometown, Ruth quickly figures out she can be Jewish or she can be popular, but she can't be both. Eager to fit in with the blond girls in the "pastel posse," Ruth decides to hide her religion. Before she knows it, she is falling for the handsome and charming Davis and sipping Cokes with friends at the all-white, all-Christian Club. Does it matter that Ruth's mother makes her attend services at the local synagogue every week? Not as long as nobody outside her family knows the truth. At temple Ruth meets Max, who is serious and intense about the fight for social justice, and now she is caught between two worlds, two religions, and two boys. But when a violent hate crime brings the different parts of Ruth's life into sharp conflict, she will have to choose between all she's come to love about her new life and standing up for what she believes.

"The story may be set in the past, but it couldn't be a more timely reminder that true courage comes not from fitting in, but from purposefully standing out." —**Jodi Picoult**

"A gorgeous story about a teenage girl finding her voice in the face of hate, heartbreak, and injustice." —**Nova Ren Suma**

"Both exquisite and harrowing ... I will hold it in my heart for a long time." —**Rachel Lynn Solomon**

ABOUT THE AUTHOR: **Susan Kaplan Carlton** currently teaches writing at Boston University. The author of *Love & Haight* and *Lobsterland*, her writing has also appeared in *Self*, *Elle*, *Mademoiselle*, and *Seventeen*. She lived for a time with her family in Atlanta, where her daughters learned the finer points of etiquette from a little pink book and the power of social justice from their synagogue.

April 2019 | Hardcover | $17.95 | 9781616208608 | Algonquin Young Readers
May 2020 | Paperback | $10.95 | 9781643750293 | Algonquin Young Readers

CONVERSATION STARTERS

1. The book opens with an epigraph that includes the line "When the wolves of hate are loosed on one people, then no one is safe." What does this phrase mean in relation to the novel? What other epigraph might work for the story?

2. Rabbi Selwick and Max both feel called to advocate for equal civil rights. What might have led them to this? In what ways do they protest or try to change society? Do you believe they are making any progress?

3. Ruth loves fashion, carefully preparing her outfits and taking note of what everyone around her is wearing. At one point, Ruth defends her interest in fashion as not shallow. Do you agree? What do these details add to the story and to your reading experience?

4. Ruth hides part of who she is to fit in with the pastel posse. Have you ever changed the way that you present yourself in order to fit in? How does modern technology like social media factor into the impulse to fit in?

5. There are a lot of different rules for societal behavior in the novel — from the pink book to Jim Crow segregation. What purpose do those rules serve in the Atlanta of the novel? In what ways do the characters follow those rules and in what ways do they break them? What rules in the 21st century, written or unwritten, work the same way for us?

6. Characters in *In the Neighborhood of True* experience various types of loss such as the loss of Ruth's father, the loss of love, and the loss of a spiritual home. How do those losses change them? How do the characters move forward?

7. The temple bombing was based on a real event, and the author's note discusses some of the ways this event echoes into the current day. In your view, how has society progressed or stayed the same since the 1958 Atlanta Temple bombing? What can we learn now from the characters in the novel and their stories?

INDIAN NO MORE
Charlene Willing McManis with Traci Sorell

Regina Petit's family has always been Umpqua, and living on the Grand Ronde Tribe's reservation is all ten-year-old Regina has ever known. But when the federal government enacts a law that says Regina's tribe no longer exists, Regina becomes "Indian no more" overnight.

Now that they've been forced from their homeland, Regina's father signs the family up for the federal Indian Relocation Program and moves them to Los Angeles. For the first time in her life, Regina comes face to face with the viciousness of racism, personally and toward her new friends.

Meanwhile, her father believes that if he works hard, their family will be treated just like white Americans. But it's not that easy. It's 1957 during the Civil Rights era, and the family struggles without their tribal community and land. At least Regina has her grandmother, Chich, and her stories. At least they are all together.

In this moving middle-grade novel drawing upon Umpqua author Charlene Willing McManis's own tribal history, Regina must find out: Who is Regina Petit? Is she Indian, American, or both? And will she and her family ever be okay?

"A beautiful and important book, honest and moving. — **Margarita Engle**, Newbery Honor-winning author of *The Surrender Tree*

ABOUT THE AUTHORS: The late **Charlene Willing McManis** (1953-2018) was born in Portland, Oregon and grew up in Los Angeles. She was of Umpqua tribal heritage and enrolled in the Confederated Tribes of Grand Ronde. She lived with her family in Vermont and served on that state's Commission on Native American Affairs. She passed away in 2018.

Traci Sorell writes fiction and nonfiction books as well as poems for children. *We Are Grateful: Otsaliheliga*, her Sibert Honor and Orbis Pictus Honor–award-winning nonfiction picture book, received starred reviews from *Kirkus Reviews*, *School Library Journal*, *The Horn Book and Shelf Awareness*. A former federal Indian law attorney and policy advocate, she is an enrolled citizen of the Cherokee Nation and lives in northeastern Oklahoma.

September 2019 | Hardcover | $18.95 | 9781620148396 | Tu Books

CONVERSATION STARTERS

1. What does Regina learn from her grandmother Chich over the course of the story? Why is Chich important to Regina and her family?

2. Why do Regina and her family have to move to Los Angeles? What is the Indian Relocation Program, and how does it affect Regina and the Petits?

3. How did Chich's stories help Regina understand herself and her identity?

4. How does Regina experience racism when she first gets to Los Angeles?

5. How do the young people in Regina's neighborhood treat and view her? How do their relationships evolve?

6. Why do you think the author Charlene Willing McManis wrote this story?

7. What did Charlene Willing McManis want to tell her readers? What is her message and why do you think that?

8. What does the title, *Indian No More*, mean to you after reading? How is the title important to understanding the entire story?

9. How does Regina grapple with her identity over the course of the book? What does she learn about herself and her family?

10. How does *Indian No More* relate to the ongoing and systematic oppression and racism that Native people experience today?

MERCI SUÁREZ CHANGES GEARS

Meg Medina

Winner of the 2019 Newbery Medal

A 2018 Kirkus Prize Finalist

A *New York Times* Best Seller

Thoughtful, strong-willed sixth-grader Merci Suárez navigates difficult changes with friends, family, and everyone in between in a resonant new novel from Meg Medina.

Merci Suárez knew that sixth grade would be different, but she had no idea just how different. For starters, Merci has never been like the other kids at her private school in Florida, because she and her older brother, Roli, are scholarship students. They don't have a big house or a fancy boat, and they have to do extra community service to make up for their free tuition. So when bossy Edna Santos sets her sights on the new boy who happens to be Merci's school-assigned Sunshine Buddy, Merci becomes the target of Edna's jealousy. Things aren't going well at home, either: Merci's grandfather and most trusted ally, Lolo, has been acting strangely lately — forgetting important things, falling from his bike, and getting angry over nothing. No one in her family will tell Merci what's going on, so she's left to her own worries, while also feeling all on her own at school. In a coming-of-age tale full of humor and wisdom, award-winning author Meg Medina gets to the heart of the confusion and constant change that defines middle school — and the steadfast connection that defines family.

"A moving coming-of-age tale. —People Magazine

"Merci Suárez has my heart." —Rebecca Stead, Newbery Award–winning author of *When You Reach Me*

ABOUT THE AUTHOR: **Meg Medina** is an award-winning Cuban-American author who writes picture books and middle-grade and young adult fiction. Her young adult novels include *Yaqui Delgado Wants to Kick Your Ass*, which won the 2014 Pura Belpré Author Award; *Burn Baby Burn*, which was long-listed for the National Book Award; and *The Girl Who Could Silence the Wind*. She lives with her family in Richmond, Virginia.

September 2018 | Hardcover | $16.99 | 9780763690496 | Candlewick Press
April 2020 | Paperback | $7.99 | 9781536212587 | Candlewick Press

CONVERSATION STARTERS

1. We see Merci taking charge almost right away in the book, leading the other girls in her class through the maintenance hallways at school to the gymnasium for picture day. But even when Merci takes the lead in this moment, she still seeks out Edna Santos's approval. How did Edna end up with so much power?

2. Merci and her brother, Roli, have to do extra community service hours as part of their scholarships to Seaward Pines Academy. Aside from having to be in the Sunshine Buddies Club, what are some of the smaller, less obvious ways that Merci notices a difference between herself and some of the other students?

3. It feels to Merci like there is suddenly a huge divide between the boys and the girls in her class, one that wasn't there when they were all still in fifth grade. Why does Merci, more than some of the other girls in her class, have a hard time adjusting to this change? How might a student who is trans or gender fluid feel about how often things are separated for boys and girls?

4. Why does a simple thing like writing an apology to Michael Clark take Merci such a long time to do? What is she worried about?

5. Merci loves snapping photos of the people around her and editing them so that the pictures show what she sees when she looks at a person. What does this tell you about Merci and the way she observes the world?

6. Over and over in the novel, Merci and the members of her family say the same thing: there are no secrets. It is the family rule. Why does this make it feel even worse when Merci finally learns the truth about Lolo's disease? Do you think her family was justified in keeping this secret and breaking their own rule? Why?

7. Meg Medina includes a lot of small clues about Lolo's Alzheimer's throughout the book. At what point could you tell something was happening with him? Why didn't Merci want to believe that something serious was going on?

THE NEXT GREAT PAULIE FINK

Ali Benjamin

An Amazon Best Book of the Month

In this highly anticipated second novel by the author of the award-winning, bestselling *The Thing About Jellyfish*, being the new kid at school isn't easy, especially when you have to follow in the footsteps of a classroom prankster like Paulie Fink.

When Caitlyn Breen enters the tiny Mitchell School in rural Mitchell, Vermont, she is a complete outsider: the seventh grade has just ten other kids, and they've known each other since kindergarten. Her classmates are in for a shock of their own: Paulie Fink—the class clown, oddball, troublemaker, and evil genius—is gone this year.

As stories of Paulie's hijinks unfold, his legend builds, until they realize there's only one way to fill the Paulie-sized hole in their class. They'll find their next great Paulie Fink through a reality-show style competition, to be judged by the only objective person around: Caitlyn, who never even met Paulie Fink.

Told via multiple voices, interviews, and other documents, *The Next Great Paulie Fink* is a lighthearted yet surprisingly touching exploration of how we build up and tear down our own myths.

"A funny and fast-paced romp." —*The New York Times*

"A book to make readers think, question, reach, laugh, and strive harder." —*Kirkus Reviews* (**Starred Review**)

"A witty, tender, and utterly engaging modern school story that draws on the wisdom of the ages." —*School Library Journal* (**Starred Review**)

"Genuinely original." —*Publishers Weekly* (**Starred Review**)

ABOUT THE AUTHOR: **Ali Benjamin** is a *New York Times* bestselling author and National Book Award finalist for *The Thing About Jellyfish*. She lives near Williamstown, Massachusetts.

April 2019 | Hardcover | $16.99 | 9780316380881 | Little, Brown Books for Young Readers
April 2020 | Paperback | $7.99 | 9780316380874 | Little, Brown Books for Young Readers

CONVERSATION STARTERS

1. Mags defines *kleos* as "Renown. Glory. Being remembered." (140) What qualities do you think make someone worthy of glory or renown? What are some examples of people who will be remembered? What would you want to be remembered for?

2. How does Caitlyn's treatment of Anna Sprang influence your view of Caitlyn as a person? Why do you think Caitlyn treats Anna the way she does?

3. In order to navigate her daily life at school, Caitlyn creates many lists of rules. Discuss how these rules impact her. Do they help, hurt, or limit her? Do you have unwritten rules in your own life?

4. The chapters switch back and forth between Caitlyn's perspective and the interviews she conducts with other characters. How do these two formats differ from each other? What kind of information does each format reveal?

5. What is the significance of the name the Originals? Is it appropriate? How do the Originals turn their uniqueness into strengths? Is Caitlyn able to do this, and if so, how?

6. What are some of the differences between Caitlyn's old school and The Mitchell School? Are there any parts that stay the same between the two schools?

7. How does the story Caitlyn tells Kiera about the girl "who felt too soft on the inside" reflect Caitlyn's own experiences? (275)

8. Henry tells Caitlyn that "Back in ancient Greece, there wasn't a single source that told the whole story of any one god, or anything else, for that matter." (332) What are some examples of characters not telling the whole story about an event or character?

9. How does Paulie's letter change your perception of him? How does the way he describes himself compare to how his classmates view him?

10. Do you think you can ever really know what someone else is going through? How can your assumptions about someone else's life impact them? How do your assumptions about others limit yourself?

STONE RIVER CROSSING
Tim Tingle

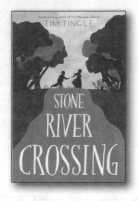

Martha Tom knows better than to cross the Bok Chitto River to pick blackberries. The Bok Chitto is the only border between her town in the Choctaw Nation and the slave-owning plantation in Mississippi territory. The slave owners could catch her, too. What was she thinking? But crossing the river brings a surprise friendship with Lil Mo, a boy who is enslaved on the other side. When Lil Mo discovers that his mother is about to be sold and the rest of his family left behind. But Martha Tom has the answer: cross the Bok Chitto and become free.

Crossing to freedom with his family seems impossible with slave catchers roaming, but then there is a miracle—a magical night where things become unseen and souls walk on water. By morning, Lil Mo discovers he has entered a completely new world of tradition, community, and . . . a little magic. But as Lil Mo's family adjusts to their new life, danger waits just around the corner.

In an expansion of his award-winning picture book *Crossing Bok Chitto*, acclaimed Choctaw storyteller Tim Tingle offers a story that reminds readers that the strongest bridge between cultures is friendship.

"Richly descriptive and leavened with humor, Tingle's complex novel offers valuable insights into rarely told history." —Publishers Weekly (**starred review**)

"Stone River Crossing *is a must read for all who know what it's like to strive to grow and learn about: freedom, friendship and fortitude.*" —**Dawn Quigley, PhD, Turtle Mountain Ojibwe Nation, author of** *Apple in the Middle*

ABOUT THE AUTHOR: **Tim Tingle** is an Oklahoma Choctaw and an award-winning author and storyteller of twenty books. In 1993, he retraced the Trail of Tears to Choctaw homelands in Mississippi and began recording stories of tribal elders. From talks with Archie Mingo emerged Crossing Bok Chitto, Tingle's first illustrated children's book. This history-based tale is the inspiration for *Stone River Crossing*. Tingle lives in Texas.

May 2019 | Hardcover | $20.95 | 9781620148235 | Tu Books

CONVERSATION STARTERS

1. How do the cultural celebrations and traditions in *Stone River Crossing* differ from your family's celebrations and/or traditions? If your family does not participate in celebrations, compare how you honor your ancestors to the traditions described in the book.

2. How might the wedding scene change if Bledsoe arrived a few hours earlier across the Bok Chitto River?

3. How does the author, Tim Tingle, describe colonization to readers?

4. How does colonization impact the storyline and your understanding of Choctaw cultures and traditions?

5. Why is it important that Lil Mo describes what his life was like at the plantation to Martha Tom? How is this essential to the book?

6. Why did the author, Tim Tingle, include Ofijo in the book?

7. Would taking the character Ofijo out of the book change the story? If so, how?

8. How does Funi Man describe iskuli (money) to Koi Losa? How does Koi Losa respond? Do you agree with how Funi Man views iskuli?

9. Imagine that the story started with Martha Tom being captured on the plantation side of the Bok Chitto River instead of Lil Mo crossing to the Choctaw Nation side of the river. How might this change the direction of the story?

10. How does *Stone River Crossing* compare to other books or short stories you have read that include Native American characters in the past, present, or future?

11. In what ways do the characters' friendships in *Stone River Crossing* relate to your friendships? Why or why not?

SUNNYSIDE PLAZA
Scott Simon

Wonder **meets** ***Three Times Lucky*** **in a story of empowerment as a young woman decides to help solve the mystery of multiple suspicious deaths in her group home.**

Sally Miyake can't read, but she learns lots of things. Like bricks are made of clay and Vitamin D comes from the sun. Sally is happy working in the kitchen at Sunnyside Plaza, the community center she lives in with other adults with developmental disabilities. For Sally and her friends, Sunnyside is the only home they've ever known.

Everything changes the day a resident unexpectedly dies. After a series of tragic events, detectives Esther Rivas and Lon Bridges begin asking questions. Are the incidents accidents? Or is something more disturbing happening?

The suspicious deaths spur the residents into taking the investigation into their own hands. But are people willing to listen?

Sunnyside Plaza is a human story of empowerment, empathy, hope, and generosity that shines a light on this very special world.

ABOUT THE AUTHOR: **Scott Simon** has won every major award in broadcasting for his personal essays, war reporting, and commentary. He has reported from all fifty states, scores of foreign countries, and eight wars. He hosts *Weekend Edition with Scott Simon* Saturday mornings on National Public Radio (which the *Washington Post* has called "the most literate, witty, moving, and just plain interesting news show on any dial") and numerous public television and cable programs. He currently resides in Washington, D.C.

January 2020 | Hardcover | $16.99 | 9780316531207 | Little, Brown Books for Young Readers

CONVERSATION STARTERS

1. How does Sal Gal perceive the world around her? What examples can you think of where she takes in the world around her through the five senses?

2. How do children react to meeting Sally and the other residents of Sunnyside Plaza? Do those reactions change based on the behavior of the adults around them and if so, how?

3. At the Passover Seder, everyone discusses the destinations of the Hebrews and other refugees. Who else in the book finds a new home or life? How do different cultures come together throughout the book?

4. Conrad explains to Sally that "sometimes, much as we love them, we just aren't the best people to be able to help the people we love." (119) What different kinds of caregiving are discussed throughout the book? How does Sally think of her mother?

5. At each stop on their journey to the police station, the residents of Sunnyside Plaza encounter different types of people. How do these people engage with the residents? What behaviors do you think made Sally and her friends feel welcomed?

6. How do the residents of Sunnyside Plaza work together? What strengths do they each bring to the table?

7. What does family mean to the residents of Sunnyside Plaza? How does this definition change over the course of the book?

8. Sal Gal is confronted by death and dying several times throughout the book. How does she cope with death? How do she and the other residents of Sunnyside Plaza grapple with what comes after death?

9. Sally maintains a very open and welcoming personality. What examples can you think of where Sally makes other people feel more comfortable? What other ways does she impact the people around her?

10. Esther tells Sally that "sometimes life puts people in front of you because you're not supposed to just walk past them" (p. 189). Which characters in the book best illustrate this idea? How can you live this in your daily life?

WE ARE HERE TO STAY: VOICES OF UNDOCUMENTED YOUNG ADULTS
Susan Kuklin

The Stonewall Honor–winning author of *Beyond Magenta* shares the intimate, eye-opening stories of nine undocumented young adults living in America.

"Maybe next time they hear someone railing about how terrible immigrants are, they'll think about me. I'm a real person."

Meet nine courageous young adults who have lived in the United States with a secret for much of their lives: they are not U.S. citizens. They came from Colombia, Mexico, Ghana, Independent Samoa, and Korea. They came seeking education, fleeing violence, and escaping poverty. All have heartbreaking and hopeful stories about leaving their homelands and starting a new life in America. And all are weary of living in the shadows. *We Are Here to Stay* is a very different book than it was intended to be when originally slated for a 2017 release, illustrated with Susan Kuklin's gorgeous full-color portraits. Since the last presidential election and the repeal of DACA, it is no longer safe for these young adults to be identified in photographs or by name. Their photographs have been replaced with empty frames, and their names are represented by first initials. We are honored to publish these enlightening, honest, and brave accounts that encourage open, thoughtful conversation about the complexities of immigration — and the uncertain future of immigrants in America.

"A must-read." —Kirkus Reviews

"We Are Here to Stay transcends politics and finds the common bonds of mankind." —Shelf Awareness for Readers

ABOUT THE AUTHOR: **Susan Kuklin** is the award-winning author and photographer of more than thirty books for children and young adults that address social issues and culture, including *No Choirboy: Murder, Violence, and Teenagers on Death Row and Beyond Magenta: Transgender Teens Speak Out*, which was named a Stonewall Honor Book. Her photographs have appeared in the Museum of the City of New York, documentary films, *Time* magazine, *Newsweek*, and the *New York Times*. Susan Kuklin lives in New York City.

January 2019 | Hardcover | $19.99 | 9780763678845 | Candlewick Press

CONVERSATION STARTERS

1. Discuss the different reasons that the young people who were interviewed and their families came to the United States. Compare the ways they initially entered the country, such as on a visa or by hiring coyotes. How did the way they arrived affect them, their families, and their experiences in the United States?

2. Education is a central value for many of those interviewed. J—– from Ghana says, "I would do anything to get back to school" (105), while G—– from Mexico believes, "Good grades are a must! If I don't do well, who knows what can happen, right?" (140) Why do they care so much about education? Why do their parents value it so highly? What kinds of problems did they face concerning college tuition because they were undocumented?

3. Y—– refers to people "railing about how terrible immigrants are." (22) Find other references in the book to prejudice against immigrants. What instances of this do you know from your own experience? Why is there so much animosity toward immigrants, both now and in the past? Read over the time line of immigration laws (161–164) and identify specific groups targeted negatively by the laws as well as those who benefited from them.

4. In the view of D—–'s sister Y—–, "The more blessings you have, the more you have to give back." (15–16) What kind of blessings is she referring to? Discuss her statement in terms of the young people in this book and in more general terms. How do different young people in the book give back, and who are they giving back to?

5. Compare parents of the undocumented young people in the book. Describe ways that some parents supported their children, financially, emotionally, and otherwise. Did the culture of the parents' birth country clash with their Americanized children? What, if any, conflicts arose as the children became more Americanized? How did the young people recognize and honor their parents' sacrifice?

BOOK GROUP FAVORITES FROM 2018

In 2019, we asked thousands of book groups to tell us what books they read and discussed during 2018 that they enjoyed most. The top titles were:

FICTION

The Great Alone
Kristin Hannah | St Martin's Press

An American Marriage
Tayari Jones | Algonquin Books

A Gentleman in Moscow
Amor Towles | Viking

The Underground Railroad
Colson Whitehead | Anchor

Carnegie's Maid
Marie Benedict | Sourcebooks

The Nightingale
Kristin Hannah | St Martin's

The Tattooist of Auschwitz
Heather Morris
Harper Paperbacks

Pachinko
Min Jin Lee | GCP

Miss Kopp Just Won't Quit
Amy Stewart | HMH

The Stars are Fire
Anita Shreve | Vintage

Sold on a Monday
Kristina McMorris | Sourcebooks

Saints for All Occasions
J. Courtney Sullivan | Vintage

(TIE — bracketed: The Stars are Fire, Sold on a Monday, Saints for All Occasions)

NONFICTION

The Radium Girls
Kate Moore | Sourcebooks

Killers of the Flower Moon
David Grann | Vintage

Hillbilly Elegy
J.D. Vance | Harper Paperbacks

Becoming
Michelle Obama | Crown

Fly Girls
Keith O'Brien | HMH

The Stranger in the Woods
Michael Finkel | Vintage

I Found My Tribe
Ruth Fitzmaurice
Bloomsbury USA

Being Mortal
Atul Gawande | Picador

Evicted
Matthew Desmond
Broadway Books

Everything is Horrible and Wonderful
Stephanie Wittels Wachs
Sourcebooks

YOUNG ADULT

The Hate U Give
Angie Thomas | Balzer + Bray

The Poet X
Elizabeth Acevedo | HarperTeen

The Book Thief
Markus Zusak | Alfred A. Knopf

I Am Not Your Perfect Mexican Daughter
Erika Sánchez | Ember

Dear Evan Hansen
Val Emmich, Steven Levenson, Benj Pasek & Justin Paul
LBYR

Love, Hate and Other Filters
Samira Ahmed | Soho Teen

Buried Beneath the Baobab Tree
Adaobi Tricia Nwaubani
Katherine Tegen Books

The Astonishing Color of After
Emily X.R. Pan | LBYR

Wonder
R.J. Palacio
Knopf Books for Young Readers

Geekerella
Ashley Poston | Quirk Books

Please visit ReadingGroupChoices.com between January 1 and April 1, 2020 to enter our 2019 Favorite Books Contest by telling us about your favorite books of 2019. You will be entered for a chance to win bookstore gift certificates to use toward your meetings plus books for each person in your group, compliments of our publishing partners.

READING GROUP
CHOICES

Selections for Lively Discussions

GUIDELINES FOR LIVELY BOOK DISCUSSIONS

1. RESPECT SPACE - Avoid "crosstalk" or talking over others.

2. ALLOW SPACE - Some of us are more outgoing and others more reserved. If you've had a chance to talk, allow others time to offer their thoughts as well.

3. BE OPEN - Keep an open mind, learn from others, and acknowlege there are differences in opinon. That's what makes it interesting!

4. OFFER NEW THOUGHTS - Try not to repeat what others have said, but offer a new perspective.

5. STAY ON THE TOPIC - Contribute to the flow of conversation by holding your comments to the topic of the book, keeping personal references to an appropriate medium.

Great Books ⁓ Great People ⁓ Great Conversation

The Spellbinding Newbery Medal Winner— Now in Paperback!

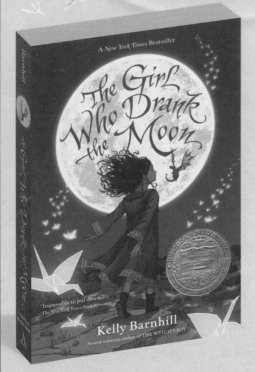

ISBN: 978-1-61620-746-5 · $9.95

A girl raised by a witch, a swamp monster, and a Perfectly Tiny Dragon must unlock the dangerous magic buried deep inside her in order to save her life, her family, and even the community that once abandoned her.

"Impossible to put down . . . *The Girl Who Drank the Moon* is as exciting and layered as classics like *Peter Pan* or *The Wizard of Oz.*"

—*The New York Times Book Review*

NEW Hardcover Gift Edition
ISBN: 978-1-61620-997-1

The *New York Times* Bestseller

An *Entertainment Weekly* Best Middle Grade Book of 2016

A New York Public Library Best Book of 2016

A *Publishers Weekly* Best Book of 2016

A Chicago Public Library Best Book of 2016

A *School Library Journal* Best Book of 2016

  Algonquin Young Readers